Critical Theory and the Anthropology of Heritage Landscapes

Cultural Heritage Studies

UNIVERSITY PRESS OF FLORIDA

Florida A&M University, Tallahassee
Florida Atlantic University, Boca Raton
Florida Gulf Coast University, Ft. Myers
Florida International University, Miami
Florida State University, Tallahassee
New College of Florida, Sarasota
University of Central Florida, Orlando
University of Florida, Gainesville
University of North Florida, Jacksonville
University of South Florida, Tampa
University of West Florida, Pensacola

Critical Theory and the
Anthropology of Heritage Landscapes

Melissa F. Baird

Foreword by Paul A. Shackel

UNIVERSITY PRESS OF FLORIDA

Gainesville / Tallahassee / Tampa / Boca Raton

Pensacola / Orlando / Miami / Jacksonville / Ft. Myers / Sarasota

First cloth printing, 2017
First paperback printing, 2022

27   26   25   24   23   22   6   5   4   3   2   1

Library of Congress Cataloging-in-Publication Data
Names: Baird, Melissa F., author. | Shackel, Paul A., author of foreword.
Title: Critical theory and the anthropology of heritage landscapes / Melissa
  F. Baird ; foreword by Paul A. Shackel.
Other titles: Cultural heritage studies.
Description: Gainesville : University Press of Florida, 2017. | Series:
  Cultural heritage studies | Includes bibliographical references and index.
Identifiers: LCCN 2017016671 | ISBN 9780813056562 (cloth) | ISBN 9780813080093 (pbk.)
Subjects: LCSH: Landscape protection. | Historic preservation. | Historic
  sites. | National parks and reserves.
Classification: LCC QH75 B2647 2017 | DDC 333.73—dc23
LC record available at https://lccn.loc.gov/2017016671

The University Press of Florida is the scholarly publishing agency for the State
University System of Florida, comprising Florida A&M University, Florida
Atlantic University, Florida Gulf Coast University, Florida International
University, Florida State University, New College of Florida, University
of Central Florida, University of Florida, University of North Florida, University
of South Florida, and University of West Florida.

University Press of Florida
2046 NE Waldo Road
Suite 2100
Gainesville, FL 32609
http://upress.ufl.edu

For Aztec

Contents

Illustrations

Figures

Maps

Foreword

Melissa Baird's *Critical Theory and the Anthropology of Heritage Landscapes* provides several case studies using archaeological, ethnographic, and archival research from fieldwork performed in Michigan, Alaska, Mongolia, and Australia. Her scholarship provides an excellent example of how practitioners can use, analyze, and deconstruct heritage landscapes within the framework of critical heritage theory (CHT). CHT is a relatively new concept in the broader field of heritage studies whereby scholars examine the sociopolitical implications and consequences of heritage. CHT connects the political and social contexts of heritage and examines the development of heritage to theories of development, postcolonial theory, rights and justice, and ecology. Baird's work investigates how knowledge and power intersect with and influence contemporary heritage practices and policies. Many professionals are working tirelessly to make CHT a distinct, viable discipline. Baird's scholarship will go a long way to help define this emerging field.

Within the framework of CHT, Baird shows how heritage landscapes are about nation-building whereby nation-states, corporations, and NGOs, to name a few, often negotiate and dictate the meaning of a place. In many cases their meanings become sanctioned through laws and policies. Baird's work shows why cultural heritage should take into consideration the perspective of Native populations and how group displacement and/or lack of representation is often the result of a lack of power. In many cases the dominant group's voice outweighs the desires of local Indigenous people. For instance, while power brokers like UNESCO aim to protect the Altai ecosystems in Mongolia, and mitigate threats to biodiversity, the people who would be most affected, the local herders, were not part of negotiations for ecosystem protection. Baird's research challenges heritage professionals to consider how their work may overlook local community concerns. In 2011 the World Heritage Convention called upon the president of the International Council on Monuments and Sites to create a working group to develop guidelines to integrate human rights considerations in World Heritage work (Ekern et al. 2012:214).

Heritage landscapes can become significant central places where citizens come to understand the relationships between past and contemporary social and political issues. Making these links between the past and the present can facilitate an exploration of both historic and contemporary concerns related to social justice (American Association of Museums 2002). Understanding the meaning of places becomes even more important, since a growing number of people are being displaced through extensive capitalist extraction or natural disasters. As extractive activities increase across the globe, new areas are opened up for development, and people and communities are removed from their traditional lands. In addition, climate change has also meant an increase of environmental disasters. Every year millions of people are displaced because of natural disasters. Ethnic nationalism, globalized forms of development, energy development, and urban renewal also threaten the heritage of millions of people. Many of these people suffer as their basic human and environmental rights are being violated. It becomes even more urgent that heritage landscapes be developed and protected to help create a sense of place for distressed populations (Oliver-Smith 2006:45–46).

Heritage landscapes represent some of the best-known places in the world, and at times they are the most contentious. As communities realize the importance of heritage landscapes they have become entangled over issues of control, access, and preservation. As Baird argues throughout her book, to truly understand heritage landscapes we must also understand their legal, political, and historical contexts. The sociohistorical contexts of a heritage landscapes have real implications for communities and nations. Baird provides an important foundational study for understanding the control of heritage landscape.

Paul A. Shackel
Series Editor

Acknowledgments

I owe my biggest debt to those who invited me onto their traditional territories, lands, and/or Country. This book would not have been possible without their permission and their generosity of time and spirit. A number of institutions provided financial or logistical support, including the Ethnic Studies and Anthropology Departments at the University of Oregon, the University of Pennsylvania Museum of Archaeology and Anthropology, Stanford University, and the Alaska Native Heritage Center in Anchorage. In addition to the agency grants listed below, research was supported by the Wenner-Gren Foundation for Anthropological Research, the National Science Foundation, and the Oregon Humanities Center. I am especially thankful to the Stanford Archaeology Center, Department of Anthropology, and the Woods Institute for the Environment, where I had the good fortune to be a postdoctoral research fellow from 2011 to 2013. I am grateful to Barton "Buzz" Thompson and Jeff Koseff of the Woods Institute for their generosity and insights. I am indebted to Lynn Meskell, a mentor and friend, who sets an example of integrity and excellence. I know this work is better because of her and my time at Stanford.

I must acknowledge all the people who have encouraged me and/or took time to provide advice, papers, and ideas: Jon Altman, Nicole Ardoin, Doug Bird, Aletta Biersack, Molly Casperson, Douglas Comer, Julie Cruikshank, Marguerite Deloney, Jen Erikson, Rachelle Gould, Valdimar Hafstein, Rodney Harrison, Ian Lilley, Arek Marciniak, Madonna Moss, Stratos Nanoglou, George Nicholas, Emma Norman, Þóra Pétursdóttir, Trinidad Rico, Kathryn Lafrenz Samuels, Sandra Scham, Phil Scher, Helaine Silverman, Laurajane Smith, Peter Vitousek, Ana Vrdoljak, the late Willem Willems, and Lauren Yapp. I owe an enormous intellectual debt to my friend and "roomie," Lindsay Weiss, whose ideas are found in this book. I have also benefited from conversations and collaborations with Rosemary Coombe. Of course, I am responsible for any errors or oversights in this work.

My work has been generously supported by a number of institutions and agencies. The National Park Service and the U.S.D.A. Forest Service supported research in Alaska from 2000 to 2005. I am grateful to Jeanne Schaaf, Terry Fifield, and Linda Yarborough for their support. Research in Lake Clark National Park and Preserve was conducted under a Cooperative Agreement (1443CA991001058). Research in Prince William Sound was supported by the U.S.D.A. Chugach National Forest in consultation with John F. C. Johnson, cultural resources manager, Chugach Alaska Corporation. A number of people provided support and/or guidance in Alaska: Don Dumond, Jon Erlandson, Dennis Griffin, David and Annette Janka (Auklet Charter Services), James Kari, Jim Keyser, Janet Klein, Carolynne Merrell, Patrick Saltonstall, Karen Steelman, Joan Townsend, and Melissa Workman. I am also deeply honored that the late Frederica de Laguna took the time to meet with me in 2002 and encouraged me to pursue my field research in Prince William Sound.

Research in Mongolia in 2006 was supported by Esther Jacobson-Tepfer. Thank-you also to Jean Bourgeois and the UNESCO WH Centre for funding my participation in the 2006 International Conference on Scythian Archaeology in Ghent and to Wouter Gheyle, Henri Francfort, and Herman Parzinger. At the ICOMOS Documentation Center, I appreciate the help of Jose Garcia, Gaia Jungelblodt, Regina Durighello, and Gwenaëlle Bourdinand. At the World Heritage Centre, I appreciate the assistance of Jens Boel, Mechtild Rössler, Junhi Han, Dieter Schlenker, Dr. Henry Cleere, and Alessandro Balsamo.

Research in Australia was supported by the Stanford Archaeology Center and Woods Institute for the Environment, two Research Excellence Fund grants and startup funds from Michigan Technological University. In Australia, a number of agencies provided material and logistical support, and people provided interviews and advice. Because of the sensitivity of some of this research, I have chosen to protect participants' anonymity. A few people I can mention here include: Mayor Peter Long, Chevron Onslow Community Liaison Officer, Jan Virgo and the Dampier Community Association, John Lally, the Aboriginal Rangers at Karijini and Murujuga national parks, Ron Critchley, CEO of Murujuga Park Council, Murujuga Aboriginal Corporation, Ngarluma Aboriginal Corporation, the Ngarluma people, Skipper Brad Beaumont, Shire of Ashburton, Yamatji Marlpa Aboriginal Corporation/ Banjima Traditional Owners. I also want to thank the Perth USAsia Centre Seed Funding Research Grant for supporting our 2014 session on resource frontiers at the Association for Critical Heritage Studies meeting in Canberra. A special thank you to Jane Lydon and fellow presenters Alistair Paterson and Aileen Walsh, for including me in your group and providing critical feedback.

I am especially grateful to Meredith Babb and Paul Shackel at the University Press of Florida for their support and patience throughout the publication process. I am particularly indebted to the anonymous reviewers who spent considerable time and energy reading and commenting on this book; their insights and feedback helped me to clarify and expand my argument.

Thank-you to ROA for permission to use his artwork and photograph of Ngarluma country for the cover. Colleagues and students at Michigan Tech have provided a welcoming community. In particular, I want to thank Val Gagnon, Hugh Gorman, Nancy Langston, Carol MacLennan, Audrey Mayer, Melissa Michaelson, Laura Walikainen Rouleau, Chelsea Schelly, Amy Spahn, Gina Stevens, Adam Wellstead, Richelle Winkler, and LouAnn Wurst.

I owe a great deal of gratitude to my friends and family. My dear friends Mary Fines, Karin Lange, and Karen DeBraal and my mother and my brother Scott have all provided a welcomed mix of encouragement and prodding. I am also thankful to my amazing stepson, Benjamin Miller, as well as his wife, Jen, and the kids, who help put things into perspective. I want to recognize my late friends Gail Jean LaTorella and Geoffrey Weitz, who provided some of my most cherished experiences of place: skipping school and exploring Salisbury Beach, Walden Pond, and the Groton woods. These carefree times with cherished friends, exploring the landscapes of New England, have served me well. But above all, I thank my husband, William "Aztec" Miller, whose love and support goes far beyond measure or description.

Prologue

Woodside's North West Shelf Visitor Centre, Karratha, Western Australia, November 2014

The view, the man told me, "does not disappoint." We are standing in the parking lot of Woodside's North West Shelf Visitor Centre looking out upon the massive onshore liquefied natural gas plant, which includes processing and domestic gas trains, condensate stabilization units, and storage and loading facilities. It is a full-sensory experience: whirring, humming, hammering, pounding, whistles, announcements, and an eternal gas flame, set against the blue hue of the Indian Ocean, which brings to mind the flags settlers once used to claim lands. Woodside built the industrial plant on the Burrup Peninsula in the Dampier Archipelago, in the Pilbara region along the northwestern coastline of Western Australia on one of the most important petroglyph and sacred sites in Australia and "Country" to the Traditional Owners, the Ngarluma/Yindjibardni, Yaburara Madudhunera, and Wong-Goo-tt-oo people.[1] The peninsula is also a biological hotspot, home to important indicator species, fringing coral reefs, protected rocky shore habitats, and, according to geologists, a place that holds evidence of the Earth's oldest life, estimated to be nearly 3.5 billion years old. Despite its universal significance, strong link to Traditional Owners, and a well-organized protest that garnered international attention and support, the majority of the peninsula is now an industrial estate.

The mid-afternoon sun is relentless, and I can tell that the interview is not going well. My interlocutor, a retired engineer on holiday, has become impatient with me. I remind myself to listen, to be courteous and polite. But instead I force the conversation back to the issues that had brought me to the Pilbara: the development rush and the impacts of mining and gas development on Country and areas with significant heritage values. The rush has emboldened extraordinary changes throughout the region: witnessed in the construction of new roads, ports, and wastewater facilities; announced by government agencies who describe their plans to build desalination plants or to bore ancient aquifers; or speculated by new streams of global capital and investment funds or cross-sector partnerships. The more obvious concerns of rapid growth—in an environmentally fragile and geographically remote region—include environmental impacts, inflation and economic inequalities, and community disruptions. Although my interviews with people throughout the region reveal that many in the community see these changes as critical to supporting economic prosperity, Aboriginal groups I had talked with found these same changes bewildering. To show the extent of changes to the landscape, I bring out photographs and maps and invite the engineer to help me locate landmarks that still remain. But instead, he politely declines and retreats to the safety of the visitor center.

Woodside's North West Shelf Visitor Centre showcases the North West Shelf Project, Australia's largest oil and gas development to date. Conceptually, its modern design draws on the ancient Pilbara landscape—the iconic red earth, rock outcroppings, and petroglyphs—and juxtaposes these with the new landscapes of energy. I ask the docent what she likes most about the design of the center, and she replies, "It represents progress." I cannot disagree, but I question what "progress" means in this context. Looking through windows etched with petroglyphs, the sight lines frame the visitor's view to take in the state-of-the-art technology (see Figure 1). At first glance, one might see the building's design and setting as a celebration of Aboriginal Country. But on reflection, I realize that a not-so-subtle shift has occurred: Country now serves as a prop to showcase energy infrastructures and technologies. In the process, Country has been transformed into a resource and the contested contexts and histories are presented as resolved.

Unlike the engineer who reveled in the grandeur of the onshore plant, I was overcome with a heaviness of heart. Whereas the engineer and docent saw progress, I saw land alienation and dispossession, a form of structural violence, a point I will develop in this book. Admittedly, my location as a white, Western scholar calls into question any real connection to the Burrup Peninsula or Aboriginal Country. Yet, I still mourned its loss. In her profoundly felt book *Living Oil*, ecocritic and scholar Stephanie LeMenager (2014:16) uses the term "petromelancholia" to describe the feelings of grief that communities have in the wake of intensive extractive processes and events. I have heard such feelings described by my interlocutors, who tell me of their struggles to rebuild in the wake of oil spills, or to adapt to rapidly changing environments. Coming to terms with loss also reminds me of scholars, sometimes years after their research was

Figure 1. View out window of Woodside's North West Shelf Visitor Centre, photo by author.

completed and the results published, who feel compelled to share experiences and concerns (see, e.g., Saulitis 2013; Slater 2002). In these cases, we see how the original mandate—the research project—shifts to something closer to memoir or testimony, and becomes an exercise in working through the difficulties and contradictions of their work, the lack of resolution, the feelings of exile and loss. This book is about such contradictions. It seeks to examine how the personal intersects with the political, to move these discussions out of the footnotes and addendums, to bring these experiences to the fore.

I

Landscapes *as* Heritage

Critical Theory and the Anthropology of Heritage Landscapes is about the sociopolitical contexts of landscapes *as* heritage. Heritage landscapes, as defined here, include urban, Indigenous, and post-industrial landscapes, wildlife management and wilderness areas, archaeological sites, coastal and marine environments, community-conserved areas, land-trust preserves, and temple complexes.[1] Landscapes figure prominently in people's lives and imaginations. As places of memory and belonging, landscapes often transcend theoretical understandings: they hold knowledge, memories, histories, songs, traumas, and so on. As the opening vignette illustrated, landscapes are also sites of conflict and crisis, displacement and loss. Such "negative" or "difficult" heritage often emerges in the wake of genocide and war, diaspora, development, and environmental disasters (after Macdonald 2009; see also Stone and Sharpley 2008; Timothy 2011). The military interventions at the World Heritage sites of Timbuktu in Mali and the Temple of Preah Vihear in Cambodia provide extreme examples (see, e.g., Meskell 2016; Silverman 2011). But perhaps less well known and equally compelling is how the heritage landscapes of Matsushima in northern Japan, designated as a Special Place of Scenic Beauty, have since become a shrine to remember people lost in the 2011 Tohuku earthquake and tsunami. What these cases all share is how landscapes become more than the scene of enactment; they are also the means by which communities negotiate identity, nation-state boundaries, or sovereignty, or by which they come to terms with difficult events. This book seeks to examine such political dynamics, cultural processes, and "frictions" (after Tsing 2005).

Landscapes are central to the business of heritage: they function as tourist attractions, entertainment venues, recreational playgrounds, respites and refuges, chronicles of historical events, and memorials and performance spaces. They also serve to legitimize identities and promote state and industry interests (see, e.g., Ringer 2013; Rojek and Urry 1997). As such, heritage landscapes are politically charged. In Rwanda, for example, the government heavily promotes its natural landscapes both to deflect attention from the national genocide and to draw Western travelers to witness these dark tourism sites (Bolin 2012). The genocide, when presented, is abstracted and simplified, occluding many of the key events and their impact on communities. This tactic is common. In a powerful anthropological and archaeological study of the town of Kimberley in South Africa, now a World Heritage site, Lindsay Weiss (2009) shows how the "big hole" left in the wake of the diamond rush was remade into a tourism site, where De Beers reinvented its own history and refashioned the mine as a tourist destination. She shows how the history of diamond mining "is delivered to a touring public according to the romantic registers of adventurisms and glitz, coolly overstepping the tens of thousands of laboring and broken bodies" (2009:40). Such historical abstractions require our attention. Shifting our focus away from *why* tourists travel to a particular place and attending instead to the *culture* of these sites should render more visible how such sites are engaged in subverting or occluding complex relationships and legacies that continue to play out in surprising ways.

This book foregrounds heritage as a site of negotiations. Heritage is a global industry that engages a network of institutions, scientists, policy experts, agencies, and practitioners who influence policy issues at local, national, and international levels. In landscape contexts, experts may provide opinions in land rights and native title claims, bioprospecting contracts, biotechnology patents, water rights and sacred sites claims, ecosystem inventories, and nominations to the World Heritage list. Such negotiations are not only technical matters but also a "cultural practice, a form of cultural politics" (Logan et al. 2015:1). Take, for example, the World Heritage cultural landscape designation developed by the United Nations Educational, Scientific and Cultural Organization (UNESCO) and adopted by the World Heritage Committee in 1992. The designation proved to be an important corrective to address the overrepresentation of Western European sites and natural heritage properties and underrepresentation of Indigenous peoples' heritage on the list (see Boer and Wiffen 2006; Cleere 2001; Fowler 2004). Yet, as I have argued elsewhere (Baird 2009), the designation also expanded what constitutes a landscape and positioned heritage managers as experts along the full heritage continuum—and in some cases, outside their expertise and qualifications. As such, ideas of heritage were largely determined through the agendas and recommendations of Western experts, international heritage agencies, and the nation-state and were reframed to fit specific World Heritage values (Baird 2009). Although disparities have changed considerably in the last decade, it is here that we see how the preoccupation with material and tangible manifestations of culture still frames how landscapes are imagined and interpreted. As Paul Lane has argued (2015), the stakes for descendant communities are high, as they are often left outside the process of knowledge production (Baird 2009; see also A. Smith 2015).

But this convergence between heritage practices and expert knowledge comes as no surprise (e.g., Carman 2005; Prosper 2007). What is new is how heritage expertise is deployed beyond the traditional heritage remit (e.g., tourism, World Heritage, National Parks) and now serves the needs of development, nation-state, industry, and other projects. Historian and heritage scholar Neil Silberman (2015:32) has argued that the nation-state draws on heritage experts (and landscapes) to validate state power. How do experts contribute to reinscribing power or creating political legitimacy? How have they addressed—or failed to address—the colonial and imperial pasts that guide and inform? Consider the new terrains of expertise, and especially how heritage experts are now applying their craft beyond the traditional contexts, such as UNESCO and the International Union for Conservation and Nature (IUCN), who today broker agreements between corporate institutions and international governing bodies such as the World Bank. The range and scope of these engagements raise fundamental questions about how expertise is deployed or shaped by political interests, disciplinary backgrounds, or corporate and donor interests (Coombe and Baird 2015). Surprisingly, such engagements have largely escaped our ethnographic attention (but see Baird 2009; Lane 2015; Meskell 2012a).

Natural heritage landscapes have received considerable attention and intersect with many of the anxieties central to contemporary debates on environmental sustainability, climate change, and resource depletion, among others. Understanding their import is even more urgent today in light of the global push to develop lands and extract resources, as well as their predicted loss due to climate impacts. At the same time, sites of natural significance have been ground zero for ongoing and contentious debates over the role of culture in conservation and development (see Agrawal and Redford 2009; Curran et al. 2009; Inglis and Bone 2006; Kopnina 2012; Redford and Sanderson 2000; Terborgh 2000). As these studies have shown, whether or not these communities thrive depends on how they are viewed—as either key drivers in environmental impacts or central to conservation approaches. Yet, implicit in many of the arguments are vestiges of the nature/culture paradigm that separates humans from nature (Baird 2015; Taylor and Lennon 2011). Although many scholars have worked to balance these limited views (see, e.g., de la Cadena 2010; Ingold 2000; Taylor and Lennon 2012), challenges remain. Recent studies have shown how the divide is situated in practice (see, e.g., Baird 2009; Meskell 2012a; Ndoro and Wijesuriya 2015) and have traced the global significance of these constructs (Lane 2015). Webber Ndoro and Gamaini Wijesuriya (2015) described in a recent study how heritage professionals working to protect conservation areas within Tsodilo Cultural Landscape in Botswana ultimately disenfranchised local communities. Much of this relates back to the muscularity of the conservation discourse, which has real consequences for communities of connection (see, e.g., Lane 2015). No matter what position one takes, how these debates play out has personal and political consequences for communities. In other words, heritage matters.

One area of concern that I will tease out in this book is the increasing centrality of extractive activities on Indigenous heritage landscapes. In Australia these contexts are not uncommon: proposed dredging related to a coal port in the Great Barrier Reef, uranium mining adjacent to Kakadu National Park, and iron ore mining in Karijini National Park. These sites are not only internationally celebrated but are also Aboriginal Country and hold important "living connections" that include genealogical, geographical, and cultural knowledge (after Sharp 2002). But as I explore in this book, extractive activities on or near Indigenous lands have become nearly ubiquitous globally. In northwestern New Mexico, for example, unconventional oil and gas development proposed in Chaco Canyon threatens to damage or destroy this important Pueblo archaeological and heritage site (Balter 2015).[2] Environmental activists have metaphorically linked arms with Native American communities to protest gas exploration in such culturally sensitive areas. Nevertheless, industry in the United States has taken advantage of the patchwork of protections and gaps between laws related to gas exploration on federal and tribal lands and those that protect tribal cultural and natural heritage resources (see H. Hoffmann 2016). Reporting from South Africa, anthropologist Lynn Meskell described how the minister of mineral resources granted a permit to mine coal within seven kilometers of Mapungubwe National Park, a World Heritage site. These examples provide a glimpse into how heritage landscapes are used to promote industry values and commitments and reveal the centrality of landscapes in industrial contexts. What remains unclear, however, is how these engagements depoliticize and/or pave the way for outsider interests, that is, how land and rights are alienated or protected through the discourses and practices of heritage. This requires our attention. How do flows of global capital related to heritage landscapes produce asymmetries, material effects, and rights violations or demote valid and pressing environmental concerns?

Although scholars have grappled with the varied political and social contexts of heritage, how to address these contexts *in* our work is not as clear. This book gives an account of how some of these challenges relate to constraints placed on how we present our work as well as the epistemological and disciplinary boundaries that in many ways shape and focus the content and context of our investigations. The cases I present serve as touchstones that show how, despite extensive research experiences and support, I lacked a venue to discuss what I encountered in the field: communities struggling with the impacts of pollution and oil spills, environmental degradation, political instability, rights violations, unfettered development, disenfranchisement, and loss. For example, I led an archaeological field project in 2005 in Prince William Sound, Alaska (see Map 2). In 1989 the region was devastated by the *Exxon Valdez* oil spill, the impacts of which were still visible during my visit. I look at my journals today and I find that most of the notes relate to the post-disaster landscapes. Yet, I did not write about these concerns in *any* reports or articles (see, e.g., Baird 2006a, 2006b). Within the contexts of developing National Register nominations, journal articles, grants and research proposals, and a master's thesis, there was nowhere to discuss or present these concerns. And although my dissertation project ultimately changed to take on these sociopolitical contexts, it required that I make significant shifts in my graduate program and develop a theoretical framework to support the new direction of my work: critical heritage studies (see Baird 2009).

Critical Heritage Studies

Critical heritage studies investigate the sociopolitical contexts of heritage (Baird 2009).[3] This comparative and cross-disciplinary framework draws inspiration from critical race and postcolonial theorists and includes insights from studies in anthropology, Indigenous studies, environmental studies, history, geography, cultural studies, public policy, and law. This approach draws from a variety of methodologies (ethnographic, archival, participatory, historical, etc.) to locate how heritage is socially and politically constructed through historical processes. It asks: What is the culture of heritage? How is heritage, as a conceptual category, doctrine, or professional practice, also the site of political struggles? My choice to frame my project in this way emerged from an attempt to engage with literatures beyond the heritage and/or archaeology remit and to place different fields in conversation, to expand what we can think in the other. For example, I drew on performance theorist Diana Taylor's (2003) work on cultural memory in Argentina and Indigenous scholars Marie Battiste and James Henderson's (2000) critique of knowledge construction to make visible the ways in which heritage was mediated within political struggles and mobilized in knowledge claims.

Delineating a genealogy of critical heritage is a difficult task and beyond the scope of this study, but it is clear that this approach owes an intellectual debt to the many activists and scholars who offered insights into how heritage is interwoven with relations of power (see, e.g., Byrne 1991, 1996; Jackson 2012; Meskell 2005; Shackel 2011; Swidler et al. 1997).[4] Antecedents would include those who have posited postcolonial critiques (e.g., Chakrabarty 2008; Fanon 1968; Said 1979), worked to address colonial legacies embedded in social science research (L. T. Smith 1999), or made room for non-Western value systems, ontologies, and epistemologies (e.g., Colwell-Chanthaphonh and Ferguson 2006, 2007; Echo-Hawk 2000; Schmidt and Patterson 1995). This list would also include those who proposed ways to create collaborative methodologies (e.g., Atalay 2012) or advocated historiographic approaches that centered non-Western peoples' concerns (Byrne 1991, 1996). More recent engagements around the politics of heritage include studies that reach beyond traditional disciplinary boundaries to engage with issues of rights (Hodder 2010; Meskell 2010); neoliberalism (Coombe and Weiss 2015); cosmopolitanism and post-colonialism (Lilley 2009; Meskell 2009; Scham 2009); race and class (Moore et al. 2003; L. Smith 2006); development (Lane 2015), and identity (Colwell-Chanthaphonh and Ferguson 2006; R. Harrison 2013). Meskell's (2012a) work on the constructs of natural and cultural heritage at National Park and Barbara Kirshenblatt-Gimblett's (1995, 2004) critique of museums' complicity in the production and "possession" of heritage are both examples of this type of work. Placed in dialogue, these very different studies expose a culture of concealment and bring into sharp relief how specific discourses are privileged in the name of safeguarding heritage.

Critical heritage approaches are informed by Laurajane Smith's (2006:4) concept of "authorized heritage discourse," the idea that a larger hegemonic discourse mediates heritage laws and practices. As such, it seeks to locate the structural contexts and questions the neutrality of heritage practices. Although Smith's argument had limitations, her critique's focus on structures (i.e., discourses, policies, and laws) and not on individual motives is appealing. Her attention to the structural dynamics made clear to me why decades-long debates around Indigenous peoples, lands, and resources had largely remained unresolved. While it is true that there have been clear gains in rights for Indigenous peoples, there still existed a disparity in access, in redressing legal infractions and in validating rights. Why have, for example, Indigenous peoples not been positioned as key decision makers? Despite highly visible and symbolic victories, or a number of significant international declarations recognizing Indigenous rights, including the Mataatua Declaration on protecting intellectual and cultural property rights, and several issued by the United Nations, including the UN Declaration on the Rights of Indigenous Peoples, passed in 2007, Indigenous communities' rights remain external to heritage negotiations. Although many scholars have successfully challenged dominant framings and provided counterhegemonic histories (e.g., Schmidt and Patterson 1995) or have advocated for ways to bridge beyond Eurocentric approaches, in many ways the disparities remained. Focusing on structural explanations for inequalities and differential access explained why the work of applied or community-based and participatory research models (see, e.g., Colwell-Chanthaphonh and Ferguson 2006, 2007; Mathers et al. 2004; Shackel 2011) seemed to take us only so far.

To be clear, *heritage* is a slippery term, and several definitions have been proposed (see, e.g., R. Harrison 2013; L. Smith 2006). For geographer David Lowenthal (1998:6), heritage is an idea that is based on values, a "declaration of faith in that past." His much-cited definition provides insights into how heritage is not history but is instead constructed through practices in the present. Others have expanded on his idea to locate how heritage is a process, a performance, or an event (Harvey 2001; L. Smith 2006). Throughout this book, I use the term *heritage* to refer to both the practices of heritage (i.e., management, interpretation, conservation) and its position as a global phenomenon and site of contestation. For me, heritage is anthropology and should not be relegated to the remit of archaeology or heritage studies. Anthropology's insistence on materiality and historically informed analyses as well as its commitment to extended ethnographic research provides a way to investigate how heritage is mobilized and mediated on the ground. Such an approach gives primacy not only to larger structures and systems at play but also to the webs of relations and signification, across time and space. As such, it is intersectional rather than hierarchical, examining the logics of heritage, how it is deployed or transgressed, as well as the narratives that underpin its claims. Anthropology's insistence on tracing historical linkages and on contextualizing local and global contexts provides unique access to investigate how heritage is mobilized and for what ends. For example, an anthropologically centered approach could trace the emergence of corporate discourse to understand how it has become reconfigured around expressions of heritage (Coombe and Baird 2015; Weiss 2014). How do different companies develop and promote heritage discourse to conduct business and/

or advance their interests? What are its cultural and political signatures? Do these differ depending on contexts (or continents), forces, and flows? How is discourse contextualized in everyday practices, and what are the consequences for local or descendant communities? Ultimately, such an approach seeks to trace entanglements, historical antecedents, and social contexts as a way to understand how value systems and meaning are produced.

The Landscape Paradigm

Like ideas of heritage, the foundation of the landscape paradigm was firmly set in Enlightenment and European cultural thinking. These movements helped to define conceptually and imaginatively that landscapes were separate from but related to human experience. Perhaps this could be an oversimplification, but it does inform how landscapes, as a modern invention, emphasized nature and cartographic space. From the earliest use of the term we can note a relationship that intentionally organizes people separate from wilderness. The Germans introduced the term *Landschaft* to denote "a collection of dwellings and other structures crowded together within a circle of pasture, meadow, and planting fields and surrounded by unimproved forest or marsh" (Stilgoe 1982:12).[5] The Dutch later adopted the term *landschap* to refer to the representation of natural scenery and, specifically, pictorial traditions that were then reproduced in maps and landscape paintings (Schama 1996). Yet, landscape geographer Kenneth Olwig (1996) sees the term as broad and encompassing humans. No matter the case, early ideas of landscape emphasized nature and cartographic space and established how people conceptualized their relationships to the world, and this would influence later understandings of how people attach meanings to place (e.g., Heidegger 1977; Ingold 1993, 1995, 2000; Taylor and Lennon 2012).

By the eighteenth and through the early twentieth centuries, the landscape paradigm shifted to focus on natural processes. In the late 1800s, geologist Sir Archibald Geikie emphasized not only scenery but also geological processes (Olwig 1996). That is, environment was the determining force with humans remaining outside, unable to mediate. To be sure, vestiges of these ideas can be seen in later conceptions of human/nature interactions that separated nature from culture or embedded culture within ideas of landscapes as a resource for capital production (see Widgren 2010:459). But, in the 1920s, geographers at the University of California would call into question such environmentally deterministic understandings to establish that human agency was central to understandings of the physical landscape. The innovative and seminal work of Carl

Sauer (1925:37) provided insights into how people shaped and understood place and would have a wide-ranging influence on the development of landscape approaches in the sciences, social sciences, and humanities (see, e.g., Kenzer 1985).[6]

In more recent times, scholars have brought considerable depth, range, and insights into the theorization of landscapes and place.[7] Scholars borrow from a wide range of social and scientific theories, philosophies, and traditions—from the structure and agency theories of Bourdieu (1977) and Giddens (1984) to general and evolutionary theories adopted from ecology, history, environmental sciences, and geography (Ashmore and Knapp 1999; Knapp and Ashmore 1999). Scholars have explored landscapes and social identities (Basso 1996; Feld and Basso 1996), the modification of land and the organization of space, human responses to environmental change, heritage land claims (Layton 1995; Taçon 1999), the memory of place (Basso 1996; Blue Spruce and Thrasher 2008; Casey 1996; Feld and Basso 1996), and Indigenous human rights (Gilbert 2010). In many cases, scholars share similar approaches. For example, landscape architects, like anthropologists or social geographers, may view landscapes as products of human ideas, values, experiences, and aspirations and may imagine landscapes as a stage—a communal and cultural arena—for transformations, memories, and activities (Anschuetz et al. 2001:165).

Yet, in many instances scholars—even within the same discipline—have widely different aims and goals. Many studies were informed by landscape approaches first developed in geography and history. Archaeologists, for example, design large-scale mapping projects to investigate land-use patterns or distribution of human activities across a landscape. A landscape historian investigating a site may focus on the functional and aesthetic aspects of the physical landscape or how the idea of place is "rooted in people's seeing of landscape" (Jakle 1987:xi). Alternatively, approached from a phenomenological perspective, a landscape architect, geographer, or anthropologist may investigate how the site was "socially produced" (after Tilley 1994:10). Each of these approaches contributes unique perspectives useful for understanding the dynamic entanglements between people and their environments. Nevertheless, the widely varied approaches, theories, and goals surrounding research and interpretation of landscapes can come at a cost. Studies can lack theoretical and methodological consistency, meaning that scholars refer to landscape with little or no "theoretical grounding" of the term (Anschuetz et al. 2001:158). Although the study of cultural landscapes has provided considerable insights into how people engage with their surroundings, the varied approaches could have a negative impact on decisions related to cultural landscapes as heritage, especially for descendant communities, a point that will be developed later. There are also concerns over misidentifying what constitutes a landscape. As scholars working in West African savanna landscapes have shown, previous understandings completely misread the landscape, which resulted in frictions and tensions within the community (Fairhead and Leach 1996; Widgren 2010).

The critical question is how (or if) studies can adapt models designed and developed for widely different contexts and data sets. For example, many scholars of anthropology are guided by theories borrowed or adapted from sociology and philosophy. To be sure, these studies provide insights into how people ascribe meaning and articulate their relationships with each other and to their physical surroundings. For example, one of the most influential and widely cited studies is by archaeologist Christopher Tilley (1994), who redirected anthropological investigations of large-scale mapping projects to focus on understanding long-term relationships between people and landscapes. He drew from the works of Heidegger and Merleau-Ponty and combined phenomenological theories with archaeological and social geographical methods to analyze how Neolithic stone monuments and tombs socialized the landscape. His innovative understanding of social memory is particularly relevant to studies of cultural landscapes, because it moves analyses away from a sometimes narrow focus on tangible material remains and activities to include intangible memories, such as narratives, stories, songs, representations, or ritual behaviors. Yet in many cases, these practices are ephemeral and/or leave few archaeological signatures; without tangible evidence or accounts, it is nearly impossible to understand how a landscape was experienced or perceived in the deep past.

Scholars have made extensive use of the interpretive possibilities opened up by studies of place and space.[8] Anthropologist Sandhya Ganapathy (2013) recently examined the concepts of place and place-making in Alaska Native landscapes and argued that how landscapes are framed has an impact not only on economic expansion but also on migration to the region. Drawing on research in Gwich'in Athabascan communities in northeast Alaska, she showed how outsiders' framings of place become embedded in legislation that prime the region for extractive resource development. In this way, we can see how culturally important places compete with what she terms "translocal framings" with far-reaching repercussions. We know in other contexts, communities compete for the right to interpret natural and cultural resources. In New Zealand, public and development interests in coastal marine areas came into direct conflict with Maori communities' customary rights (Ruru 2009; Strack 2014). Maori define their interests in foreshore and seabed areas based on cultural and customary rights and land tenure; these rights can be eroded when interpreted through common or statutory rights. As New Zealand geographer Mick Strack (2014) has argued, it is crucial that parties engaged in conflicts find resolution, because despite widely different interpretations, these same coastal areas are critical to mitigating coastal hazard risk due to sea-level rise. We might ask: How do different decision makers and agencies vary in their goals and mandates related to land management and conservation? How do stakeholders' needs and cultural backgrounds influence protection of heritage landscapes, and what are the implications?

As I argue later in this book, the multiple theories and methods that are brought to bear in interpreting cultural landscapes, what I refer to as the "epistemologies of landscapes," intersect with issues related to cultural and natural heritage, landscape preservation, and identity. Although developments within the landscape paradigm have enabled greater flexibility in design and practice, the position, theoretical training, and goals of a researcher often direct the focus and outcome of a study. Although scholars may share similar approaches—for example, anthropologists or social geographers who both view landscapes as products of human ideas, values, and experiences—in many instances scholars have very different methods, even if they work within the same discipline. An archaeologist, for example, may investigate how the symbolic practices are part of a distribution of material culture and meaning, whereas a landscape architect may focus on the functional and/or aesthetic aspects of the standing stones and petroglyphs. In contrast, a geographer or anthropologist may consider how the site was a place of cultural production. At the same time, a landscape ecologist or conservation biologist may focus instead on species' interactions or the health of the region's ecosystems. Each of these approaches undoubtedly contributes something to our understandings of the dynamic relations between people and place. Yet, as many scholars have shown, Indigenous and descendant communities may not view landscapes in the same way (see, e.g., Baird 2009; Byrne 2003a). The widely varied approaches, theories, and goals surrounding research and interpretation of landscapes may come at a cost. Although the study of cultural landscapes can provide considerable insights into how people engage with their surroundings, what I want to make clear is that the varied approaches could have a negative impact on decisions related to cultural landscapes as heritage, a point that will be developed later.

Equally important is that we are attentive to the shadow side of landscapes, the segregated spaces, or landscapes of risk, criminality, and war (see, e.g., Byrne

2003a, 2003b; Logan and Reeves 2008). A growing body of research has shown how landscapes become sites of power and control or are policed, demarcated, and inscribed with notions of difference (Casella 2007; Coombes 2003). Norwegian scholars Marek Jasinski, Marianne Soleim, and Leiv Sem (2009), for example, have demonstrated how traumatic experiences of war are embedded in cultural landscapes, not only through material heritage but also by intangible connections that have been largely erased from the national narrative of resistance. They propose that studies must include such painful heritage not only as a way to include the politics of collective memory but also to help reframe how heritage is presented (see, e.g., Byrne 2003b). I would add that locating landscapes of disenfranchisement or loss is increasingly urgent today, as we see a merging and blending of corporate and Aboriginal conceptions, urban and colonial, and industrial and environmental landscapes that work to obscure sociopolitical contexts that include rights violations, socioeconomic disparity, and subjugated histories. Such contexts are significant. What I suggest here is that our studies bring in historical depth and trace the undercurrents of the power, how these are taken up and reconfigured, and to mark the changes in tone, and make these legible.

Research Methods and Outline of the Book

Material for this work is based on archaeological, ethnographic, and archival research conducted during fieldwork in Alaska between 2000 and 2005, in Mongolia in 2006, and in Australia in 2012, 2014, 2015, and 2016. These experiences include cultural landscape and archaeological work in coastal areas of Prince William Sound and Cook Inlet, Alaska (see Map 2); an ethnographic and cultural landscape survey in the Altai Mountains of Mongolia (see Map 3); an ongoing ethnographic project in Western Australia; and in-depth archival and ethnographic work in Belgium, France, and Canada. I also draw on my experience as an international heritage expert for UNESCO and as the NAGPRA coordinator at Agate Fossil Beds National Monument, where I worked with 28 federally recognized tribes on issues of reburial and repatriation, proposed archaeological research, and examined the effects of this research on traditional cultural properties (see Baird and Knudson 2012).

This book is composed of four themed chapters. Chapter 2 describes my dissertation research on one of the UNESCO World Heritage cultural landscapes, Uluṟu–Kata Tjuṯa in Australia, to demonstrate how state and national laws and World Heritage and national park policies work in ways that force Traditional

Owners to make claims within systems that are largely incompatible with their custodial responsibilities, knowledge practices, and customary laws. I show how largely apolitical and ahistorical narratives reconfigured the historical and social conditions of the park and redefined Traditional Owners' relationship to Country. Chapter 3 considers the environmental contexts of cultural landscapes in coastal sites in Alaska (*Exxon Valdez* oil spill; see Map 2) and Mongolia (climate change; see Map 3) as a way to think through how this unique type of heritage intersects with and shapes environmental concerns and contexts. I argue that the sociopolitical contexts must hold a more prominent position in ongoing debates on environmental sustainability. In chapter 4, I discuss the culture of expertise in heritage negotiations. I argue that the "epistemologies of landscapes" interfere with and shape identities in ways that have not been examined. Chapter 5 presents my most recent research on the resource frontiers of Western Australia. I argue that the global mining and gas industries are mobilizing the language of heritage, Indigenous rights, and sustainability in their conceptions of heritage through their corporate and social responsibility campaigns. I point to the urgency in making clear the competing claims and tracing the varied agendas of global institutions, corporations, the nation-state, and stakeholders. The book concludes with some recommendations for how engagements with landscapes can include emancipatory discourse and/or are deployed in ways that mobilize agency and make room for multiple understandings.

2

The Politics of Place

Uluru–Kata Tjuta National Park, Australia

When people say, "oh we lost this land or we lost that land," we didn't
lose it anywhere. . . . The problem is that we haven't been given the power
in the non-Aboriginal legal system to fulfill the custodial right. . . . [U]ntil
that consent is properly given, then we still live under bad laws.

Dennis Walker (quoted in Watson 2009:27)

According to Deborah Bird Rose, to understand Country "is to know the story
of how it came into being" (1996:36). *Country* is the term Aboriginal peoples use
to describe their ancestral and inherited places and the practices or laws that
guide behavior. Country holds the knowledge of Law, and caring for Country is
how people steward the land, including visiting sites, conducting ceremonies,
and maintaining knowledge. Central to this philosophy is the Dreaming, or
Law, creation stories that link ancestral beings with contemporary and future
generations (D. B. Rose 1996). These stories also tell how these beings emerged
from places on the land, the sea, and the sky and "assum[ed] the bodily forms of
various humans, animals, birds and plants. . . . They were shape-changing beings
with immense power, who travelled across the land and sea, performing great
deeds of creation, and now lie quiet in focal points on the landscape" (Flood
2006:98). Dreaming, like Country, mediates Aboriginal peoples' cultural and
spiritual practices: Both are tied to places in the land.

This chapter describes Uluru–Kata Tjuta National Park, a sacred Aboriginal landscape managed in collaboration with the Traditional Owners, known
collectively as Anangu, located in the southwest of Northern Territory in
Central Australia (see Map 1). I anchor this chapter in Country. Anangu's
knowledge of Country can be traced to the "Dreaming" or "Dreamtime," and
their oral narratives of place-names, patterns in the landscapes, waterholes,
and animal beings indicate that they originated from the Uluru monolith.
Uluru is Country to Anangu and is the philosophy of Tjukurpa, or the Law,

and defines and governs all aspects of their lives, including religion, moral systems, law, creation stories, and relationships to ancestors, plants, animals, and people. Tjukurpa is a "living philosophy" (Kerle 1993:14) and includes reciting place-names, managing the landscape with fire, maintaining water sources, and singing the traditional *inma* song cycles. The Law restricts access to and knowledge of sacred sites to certain members. This knowledge guides relationships to land, to others, and to all forms of life. "People talk about Country in the same way they would talk about a person" (D. B. Rose 1996:7–8). People follow strict protocols when traveling and seek permission to enter other groups' Country (Myers 1982). European colonizers ignored or misunderstood such obligations. They brought with them preconceived and largely inflexible ways of viewing the world, ways that were incompatible with these protocols and views (Kerwin 2006; D. B. Rose 1996).

Heritage landscapes as Country are often sites of dispossession and loss. This

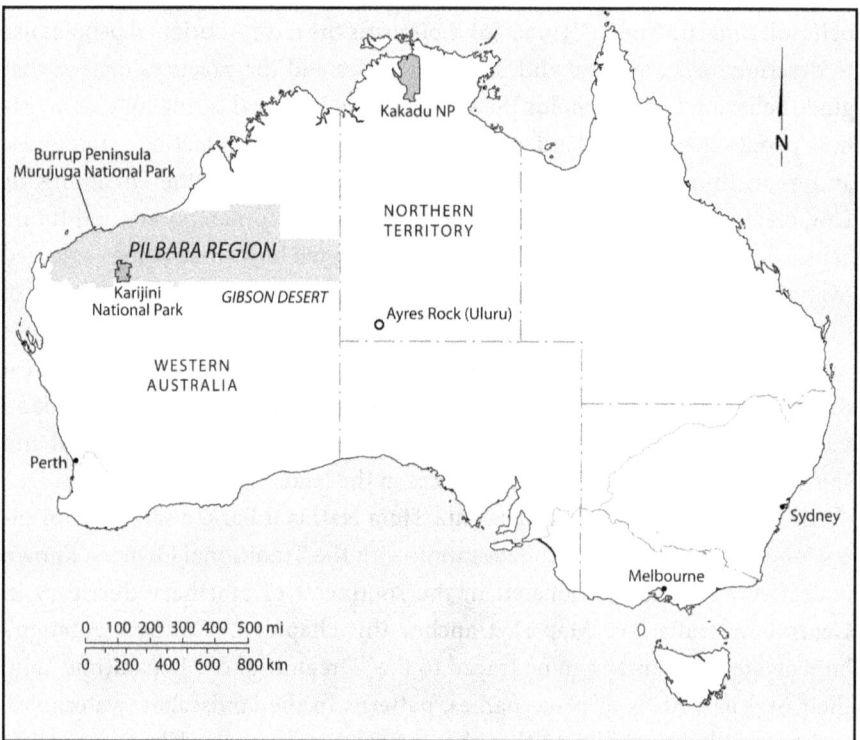

Map 1. Australia with principal field sites, map by Bill Nelson.

chapter shows how the histories of land alienation, often occluded in heritage management contexts, have far-reaching impacts on a community's claims to their traditional homelands, resources, and/or subsistence practices. I focus on the history of Uluṟu–Kata Tjuṯa National Park, a sacred Aboriginal landscape managed in collaboration with the Traditional Owners. Designated a national park in 1977, it was listed as a natural World Heritage property in 1987 and as a World Heritage cultural landscape in 1994. This chapter presents the historical, cultural, and legal contexts of Uluṟu–Kata Tjuṯa's nomination to the World Heritage list to demonstrate how the politics of the past informs the management of cultural landscapes in the present. I do not present an exhaustive overview of the history of events or a detailed description of ethnographic data, as those are described elsewhere (Baird 2009). Instead, I take as my central point of interest the largely apolitical and ahistorical narratives of the park that occlude the historical and social conditions of the park that I see as redefining the Traditional Owners' relationship to Country. Locating Aṉangu's relationship to Country within their historical experience of colonialism will bring into relief how the legacies of these early encounters are embedded in land-management practices today and how the struggle is rooted in the control of Country.

Aboriginal Country and the Doctrine of *Terra Nullius*

Australian nation-building was founded upon the doctrine of *terra nullius*, a Latin term meaning "vacant land" or "land belonging to no one" (Borch 2001; Connor 2005; Flood 2006; Watson 2009), which sanctioned European "colonists and ex-convicts" to claim Aboriginal lands "virtually free of charge" (Kercher 2002:102). Aboriginal scholar Irene Watson (2002:254) viewed *terra nullius* as justifying "violence, in all its forms, rendering our life and our laws pre-historic, invisible, un-evolved in time." This new order allowed for and legitimized the sovereignty of the Crown and protected governments from having to recognize or compensate Aboriginal peoples (Fletcher 1999). Ultimately, the doctrine transferred the power to own and speak for Aboriginal lands to European colonists and made it easier for them to impose their ideas of land use and land ownership. In the process, Aboriginal peoples' obligations and responsibilities to care for Country were ignored.

By the 1800s and throughout much of the twentieth century, the colonies, states, and (after 1901) the newly formed Commonwealth, prevented Aboriginal people from exercising their rights to their traditional lands through a series of laws and policies aimed at assimilation (Armitage 1995; Havemann 1999). The Aboriginal Protection Act of 1909, for example, forced Aboriginal people to leave their lands and move to reserves and settlements. The Commonwealth promoted the law as a protective measure for Aboriginal people, but it effectively established the institutional framework that divested them of their lands. In the reserves they were forced to adopt Western land-use practices. This punitive system not only limited their employment opportunities, representation in government, and access to citizenship but also restricted travel to sacred sites. Anthropologist Robert Layton (1986:76) deemed settlement a "planned step in the breaking down of the tribal spirit."

Northern Territory representatives were particularly harsh (Peterson and Sanders 1998). Beginning with the Northern Territory Aboriginals Act in 1910, they established control over the welfare of Aboriginal people through policies that aimed to divest them from their lands. In 1911 the Northern Territory Aboriginal Ordinance passed, which restricted where Aboriginal people could live, made vagrancy a crime, and imposed a permit system for travel. The thrust of this ordinance was not only to minimize interactions but also to govern the activities and movement of Anangu. The legacy of such restrictive policies would be felt for years to come. Also in 1911, Northern Territory became autonomous from the South Australia Commonwealth jurisdiction, and Chief Protector Baldwin Spencer established reserves to prevent "interferences" between Aboriginal and whites and to encourage Aboriginal people to move to settlements (Chesterman and Galligan 1997:143). In 1918 the Commonwealth passed the Aboriginals Ordinance, which forced unemployed Aboriginal people onto reserves and restricted travel, which amounted to "requiring passports" to travel to and care for Country (Chesterman and Galligan 1997:145).

Australian courts did not recognize Aboriginals' land titles, sovereignty, or customary laws and did not grant citizenship until the Referendum of 1967. Before that, the Australian states determined and implemented rights. The unevenness of the courts was evident in how Australian courts applied "aboriginal customary law" to decide conflicts but used Commonwealth or state laws to determine land claims involving non-Aborigines (Kercher 2002:100). As a result, Aboriginal people had no legal recourse to present land-right claims. Aboriginal scholar Aileen Moreton-Robinson (2003:79) argued that these policies made "whiteness the definitive marker of citizenship," thus denying access to Indigenous people. In this context, "whiteness" is less about a physical characteristic than it is about citizenship that bestows power, rights, and access to resources. "Australian law seems to have incorporated and accommodated the settled native as 'British subject,'" Watson (2009:28) wrote, but in truth, "Aboriginal peoples were treated as enemies and objects of British law." In this way, Aboriginal people were marked as non-citizens, denied access to their traditional lands and resources, and positioned as subjects of the Crown, far from their Aboriginal systems of law and authority (see Byrne 1996). And, of course, these restrictive policies created a hierarchy of rights and powers tied to land.

By the late 1960s, Aboriginal groups organized to reclaim rights and lands. In 1966, Aboriginal stockmen gained national attention and ignited a social movement in their protests for better wages and conditions at Wave Hill, a cattle station in Northern Territory. The Mirrar, the Traditional Owners of Kakadu National Park, also organized and mobilized against the Commonwealth and Territory governments, which supported expanding a uranium mine. The Mirrar played an active role in shaping legislation that led to the authorized joint management of park lands, the model, described later, that Uluru–Kata Tjuta National Park was based on (see De Lacy and Lawson 1997).

A major shift that recognized Aboriginal rights occurred in 1976, with the passing of the Aboriginal Land Rights (Northern Territory) Act (ALRA), which granted traditional lands to Aboriginal groups, though claims were limited to lands not owned by the Crown. This law was the result of the tireless effort by Indigenous peoples to have their rights to lands recognized by the Crown. Nevertheless, Aboriginal interests remained tied to national interests. Despite a strongly held belief that statutory land rights already provide for and protect Aboriginal peoples' care for Country (Watson 2009), in 1979 the Parliament passed the Aboriginal Sacred Sites Act. This law established the Aboriginal Sacred Sites Protection Authority and placed protection of sacred sites under Commonwealth control. As we will see, these land-rights laws would be amended and weakened.

A new wave of Aboriginal rights movements ignited in the early 1980s. In 1982, Torres Strait Islander Eddie Koiki Mabo and four others petitioned the High Court of Australia for recognition of his traditional lands, Mer (Murray Island) (Sutton 2003). In this landmark native title case, Mabo argued that his people had lived on and exclusively possessed these lands and that therefore they were the true owners. He acknowledged that the British Crown had exercised sovereignty when it annexed the islands but claimed that his people's rights had not been validly extinguished. It would take a decade for the High Court of Australia to weigh in, and in June 1992 the Court decided in favor of Mabo and ruled that the treatment of Indigenous property rights based on the principle of *terra nullius* was racist. The High Court's Mabo decision was the "first time Aboriginal and Islander people's ownership of country [had] been formally and publicly acknowledged" (D. B. Rose 1996:19), and it established Indigenous groups as the rightful owners of their ancestral lands that settlers had taken. Today, each native title case is considered within the traditions and customary law of the Aboriginal owners of the land or Country. In spite of this, Watson (2009:30) has maintained that the Court missed the "opportunity to review and heal the unlawful foundations of Australia . . . but instead it affirmed the fiction of a lawful and peaceful settlement." Watson (2009:35–36) contends that the Australian state did not truly intend to protect or empower Traditional Owners, and that native title laws reorganized Aboriginal title into Australian property law.

Aboriginal heritage was also central to negotiations and worked in ways antithetical to Aboriginal peoples' cause. In 1983 the Commonwealth passed the World Heritage Properties Conservation Act. This act was rushed through in response to the nominated Tasmanian World Heritage site, and it was challenged by representatives of the Tasmanian government because they saw it as a breach of their state's rights and not part of the Commonwealth's jurisdiction. The Commonwealth responded that it "could enact domestic legislation in relation to 'external affairs,'" as Laurajane Smith (2006:186) noted, and for "purposes of meeting an international treaty—in this case the UNESCO Convention for the Protection of the World's Cultural and Natural Heritage." The Commonwealth sought protection for properties on the World Heritage list, and also for "purposes of protecting Aboriginal heritage" (2006:186), but I suspect that this act was also a political move to demonstrate to the World Heritage Committee that Australia was a key player in heritage preservation. The act was challenged and was repealed in 1999, replaced with the Environment Protection and Biodiversity Conservation Act, described later. Despite protests from multiple stakeholders, including archaeologists, Traditional Owners, environmentalists, politicians, hydroelectric representatives, and Tasmanian officials, the Commonwealth ignored these and extended their authority to establish the site as an internationally significant World Heritage site. These tensions illustrate how different stakeholders maneuver and negotiate to support, justify, or refute claims to heritage landscapes. Most importantly, we see how the legal apparatus and overarching political authority frustrate Aboriginal peoples' attempts to self-determination and determine their relationship to land.

In 1984 a stopgap measure to protect Aboriginal cultural heritage was put forward until comprehensive land-rights and heritage protection legislation could be passed (Central Land Council 2003). The Commonwealth passed the Aboriginal and Torres Strait Islander Heritage (Interim Protection) Act, aimed to protect sites and objects of traditional significance. But in just two years the act was amended and placed protection of sacred sites under ministerial discretion, effectively weakening the Traditional Owners' rights (Central Land Council 2003). In these machinations we see that Aboriginal consultation was never a priority: Northern Territory established a committee to make recommendations regarding Aboriginal sacred or significant areas, but no Aboriginal people were included on the committee. The Commonwealth and Northern Territory eroded the legislative power meant to protect Aboriginal people's claims to their lands, making it even more difficult for them to carry out their obligations to Country.

Nevertheless, the Native Title Act, passed in 1993, set precedent for Aboriginal groups to establish their traditional law and ownership of their lands. It was groundbreaking in that it allowed Indigenous Australians to claim their traditional territories that were not owned by the Crown. Native title is literally grounded in the land and "[translates a] primarily spiritual connection to land into proprietary rights and interests, requiring proof of the connection that a particular Indigenous society has under traditional laws and customs" (Anker 2007:vi, 7). To address native title claims under the direction of the Federal Court of Australia, the Commonwealth established the National Native Title Tribunal the following year. Yet not all are convinced that native title provides protections. Watson (2009:40) maintained that native title "is a process that more frequently results in a loss to Aboriginal Traditional Owners than in an advancement in Aboriginality." She is arguing that the process of native title is part of the larger colonial and assimilation project that expands the authority of non-Aboriginal people into matters of Aboriginal peoples' care of Country. Although this view is not shared by all (e.g., Lokan 1999), Watson does raise an important question: Does native title interfere with or disrupt Traditional Owners' custodial responsibilities to Country, or does it misinterpret the nature of these relationships? This is an important point to think about in relation to how the management of heritage landscapes may also interfere or disrupt such connections.

The "bad laws" that Dennis Walker referred to in the epigraph of this chapter are those that originate from non-Aboriginal legal systems. That is because these laws do not recognize Traditional Owners' existing systems of law and authority or their obligation to Country. Clearly, the "state" comprises a diverse range of stakeholders with a diversity of philosophies, motivations, agendas, and allegiances, which, in many cases, interfere with or prevent Aboriginal peoples' care of Country. Ultimately, the doctrine of *terra nullius* removed the responsibility of European colonizers to recognize Aboriginal peoples' custodial responsibilities to Country. With each law, policy, ordinance, and ideology the state solidified this doctrine with laws and policies that marked Aboriginal people as subordinate groups without rights to their lands. As I see it, the legacies of restrictive assimilation policies and the *terra nullius* doctrine persist in land-management practices today. Country was imagined by Anangu, denied by Northern Territory, and reimagined by the Commonwealth, the parks system, and the World Heritage community. Despite their move to regain control of their lands, Anangu's knowledges and practices were managed within rigid legal and governmental systems that ignored their systems of authority. As I argue, the struggle among these groups is rooted in the control of Country.

"Keeping the land of our fathers"

The history of physical dispossession began when, in 1873, explorer W. C. Gosse climbed the Uluru monolith and renamed it Ayers Rock, after the chief secretary of South Australia, Sir Henry Ayers. Gosse wanted to claim the site before his colleague and competitor W. E. P. Giles did. In a letter to the surveyor-general of South Australia, Gosse explained, "I was compelled to turn south, crossing Mr. Giles' track several times, the eastern arm of his Lake Amadeus, and on to a high hill, east of Mount Olga, which I named Ayers Rock."[1] Gosse, like Giles and other explorers, settlers, mapmakers, and adventurers, traveled the Australian landscape, renaming its landforms, rivers, plains, and deserts, and in the process effacing Indigenous peoples' histories. Renaming is a colonial act that dispossesses people from their lands and reorganizes their geographies. Mapmaking, as anthropologist Suzana Sawyer (2004:55) reminds us, is "an inherently political social practice." Renaming erases the histories of a place and denies the stories of those to whom it belongs. For the Anangu this renaming translated in their lands being redistributed, which handicapped their efforts to explain their specific rights, heritage, and identities.

This section presents a broad sketch of the historical background related to Anangu's struggles for land rights and the 1985 leaseback of Uluru–Kata Tjuta. I rely on heavily on Robert Layton's (1986) and Graham Griffin's (2002) rich historical research of the park and other historical evidence to examine the relationship between Anangu and the Commonwealth and Northern Territory to illustrate how changes in these relationships mirrored changes occurring within the self-determination movement in Australia in the 1970s. The appendix to this volume presents a broad chronology of these events. This section also describes how Uluru—known as the "red center"—also became a potent symbol in white Australians' search for national identity. Ultimately, we see how the tourist industry and Northern Territory appealed to these strongly held beliefs in their efforts to prevent the leaseback of the park to the Traditional Owners.

As described, the Commonwealth adopted policies to encourage Aboriginal people to assimilate and established reserves to provide "security" and, in some sense, to control where Indigenous groups lived and worked. What are not typically acknowledged were the economic interests tied to Aboriginal lands: prospecting, pastoralism, hunting, and mining (Griffin 2002). Reserves were largely viewed as ways to govern interracial contact and minimize conflict, but they only exacerbated Aboriginal peoples' mistrust of the government. In many cases, reserves were located hundreds of kilometers from traditional lands. In 1920, for example, Northern Territory established the Petermann Aboriginal Reserve under the Northern Territory Crowns Lands Ordinance and required Aboriginal people to move away from developing towns and grazing lands to the east (Arnold and Arnold 2003). Later, Northern Territory reduced the reserve to accommodate expanding gold exploration and cattle farming. It is important to stress that despite movement to reserves and threat of arrest or harm, Aṉangu continued their care of Country and traveled and conducted ceremonies (Griffin 2002:364–35). Numerous observations by early explorers and travelers from the late 1800s to the 1930s showed that sizable groups of Aboriginal people conducted ceremonies and gathered at what are today known as sacred sites (Layton 1986:35–37, Table 3).

By the 1930s increased visitor access to the area was facilitated by motorized vehicles, and the Northern Territory and local governments responded quickly to minimize Aṉangu's contact with tourists. By the 1940s, Ayers Rock was a destination. Much of this can be attributed to H. H. Finlayson, the director of the South Australian Museum, who brought national attention when he petitioned the government to protect it as a national park. Not long after, a series of articles published about Uluṟu in *Walkabout* magazine drew a narrative around a bush mythology (Griffin 2002:365). Uluṟu was no longer only of interest to rugged explorers and scientists; now it had captured the imagination of non-Indigenous Australians. Traveling to the iconic desert landscape became tied to Australians' national identity. Jane Carruthers (2003:243) argued that this connection was forged in the search for a "new notion of 'Australianness.'" Uluṟu—literally and geographically—anchored the continent and became a beckoning symbol for Australians.

With mounting pressures from tourist interest groups and local tourist operators, the Commonwealth declared Ayers Rock a national park in 1950, and in 1958 both Ayers Rock and Mount Olga were removed from the Petermann Aboriginal Reserve to form the Ayers Rock–Mount Olga National Park. Not surprisingly, Aṉangu were not consulted. The federal minister for Aboriginal

Affairs argued that this was because the region "now had little ceremonial significance for the natives" (Griffin 2002:365), while Northern Territory officials claimed that "aboriginal people had lost interest in it as a traditional site" (Carruthers 2003:243–244). Clearly this was not the case, and what is more likely is that Northern Territory prevented Anangu from visiting the site to appease the local tourist operators who had lobbied the national and territorial governments to minimize Anangu presence.

Economic incentives were not typically discussed in negotiations for the use of the lands or creation of the park. Northern Territory's economy was increasingly tied to tourism, and communities outside the park came to rely on the revenue. In the late 1950s the park built infrastructure to accommodate overnight visitors. But, of course, they had to ensure that the park was presented in their terms. Representatives of Northern Territory Native Welfare Branch became increasingly uncomfortable with the "image of ragged Aboriginals selling artefacts and begging around" and discouraged Anangu from visiting or camping in the park (Layton 1986:86). To resolve this, the Commonwealth revoked Anangu's pastoral subsidies, which forced them to move back to the park. Heated interactions between Anangu and tourists increased, and the tourist industry lobbied the Native Welfare Branch to move Aboriginal people away from the park. Some Anangu refused to leave, and many were forced to seek work throughout Central Australia or make artifacts to sell to tourists (Layton 1986:86). The campaign to remove Anangu, or at least to minimize their presence, was mostly successful, and by 1962 only sixty Anangu were living in the park. Just a few years later, camping facilities were present, but no recorded Anangu (Layton 1986:76). Although Anangu were not prevented from visiting the park, the Native Welfare Branch made it nearly impossible for them to stay, having establishing their authority to speak for and control Anangu's Country through the force and power of the state.

The relationship between managers and Anangu improved somewhat in the late 1960s, and Anangu were allowed to visit a few sacred sites (Layton 1986). However, neither Northern Territory nor Parks Australia acknowledged Anangu's claims to the land and resources, and Anangu were "repeatedly forced to seek piecemeal concessions from the authorities" (Layton 1986:97). This is an important point that persists in land-management practices to come. At the same time, Anangu were also frustrated because managers allowed tourists to photograph and access their sacred sites. In these interactions, we see how Anangu were marked as outsiders and forced to negotiate punitive and restrictive policies aimed at preventing their care of Country. After all, until the Referendum in 1967, Anangu, like other Aboriginal people throughout Australia, were not considered citizens.

Not to be deterred, by the 1970s some Anangu had moved back to reserves surrounding the park, though the Commission of the Northern Territory, formerly the Northern Territory Reserves Board, vehemently opposed this (Griffin 2002:365). Anangu's struggles to reclaim their ancestral lands were part of a larger movement for sovereignty and self-determination that was gaining momentum throughout Australia. By 1972 the Commonwealth shifted its official policies from assimilation to self-determination. That same year, under Northern Territory legislation, Anangu incorporated and became the Uluru Community, and Traditional Owners performed the first recorded ceremonies at Uluru (Layton 1986). The Native Welfare Branch assisted Anangu in building a store to sell goods and gasoline to the increasing number of tourists to the region.

Anangu became increasingly vocal about tourists desecrating their sacred sites, and in 1973 they established the Ayers Rock Advisory Committee to address their concerns. That same year, the Federal House of Representatives Standing Committee on Environment and Conservation visited the park to prepare a status report (Layton 1986). The committee met with "white tourist operators and conservation experts" and members of Aboriginal groups from the Mimili, Ernabella, and Docker River communities (Layton 1986:94). One Anangu elder reported that he feared white people because of the mistreatment and alleged killing of his brother. He discussed the spiritual significance of Uluru and the importance of access to areas of the monolith that had been closed to his people. The committee's report noted that rights of the Traditional Owners must be ensured and suggested that an advisory committee with Aboriginal members be established and that the park employ Aboriginal rangers. At the same time, the report noted the importance of Ayers Rock to white Australians.

In 1975 the Australian National Parks and Wildlife Service took over supervision of Uluru from Northern Territory authorities. Anangu were pleased to sever their connection to Northern Territory and, as Carruthers (2003:246) argued, knew that the "Federal Government would be more sympathetic than the Northern Territory." In 1976, committee members revisited the park, but most Anangu elders did not attend, in part, because they were tired of having to repeatedly state their position. As one interpreter noted (quoted in Layton 1986:98), "the older people in particular feel they have said all that needs to be said: they do not wish to go over the same ground again." Moreover, senior men were outraged that they would have to make a claim for their traditional lands, because "for about five years the Federal and Territory Governments had regularly consulted them as if they were the area's Aboriginal owners" (Layton 1986:99).

The committee asked the Central Land Council and Department of Aboriginal Affairs to prepare reports and discuss the importance of the park with Traditional Owners, especially in light of plans to divide the park. The meeting was not well attended. In the report, however, senior men and women asserted that dividing the park would interfere with their responsibility to care for Country. They were not against tourism per se, but wanted to have their rights to Country met and to receive better housing and permission to camp without restrictions (Layton 1986:98–100). The park appointed three Aboriginal rangers, but they were assigned menial jobs, such as emptying trash and cleaning bathrooms (Layton 1986:96).

When the park was declared part of the Commonwealth National Parks system in 1977, the director of Australian National Parks, Dr. Derrick Ovington, visited the park and tried to meet with the Traditional Owners. Managers assumed they would be available, but the meeting was not well attended, with senior Anangu men sending younger men as proxies (Layton 1986:98–99). A bit of backstory explains their absence. Anangu were uneasy that the Northern Territory (Self-Government) Act would be passed and would return control of the park to Northern Territory (Layton 1986:99). The Commonwealth decided to reserve the park for the National Parks and Wildlife Service, and the title was vested in the director of the Australian National Parks and Wildlife Service, though from 1978 until 1985 the park was managed by officers of the Northern Territory's Parks and Wildlife Service.

Traditional Owners, the Pitjantjatjara Council, and the Central Land Council lobbied Prime Minister Malcolm Fraser and Aboriginal Affairs minister Fred Chaney to amend the Aboriginal Land Rights Act (NT) to allow an Aboriginal land claim. Between 1979 and 1983, Anangu and the Commonwealth negotiated for title of Uluru–Kata Tjuta. Anangu disagreed with the Commonwealth's proposal to establish an advisory committee in which Anangu would make recommendations on park management and instead advocated for joint management (De Lacy and Lawson 1997; Uluru–Kata Tjuta Board of Management/ANPWS 2000:9). Northern Territory wanted the title of Uluru transferred from the Commonwealth to Northern Territory, which would have given some rights, but not control, of title to the Traditional Owners (Central Land Council 2003). In 1979 the Central Land Council, acting on behalf of the Traditional Owners, submitted a claim for Uluru and adjoining Crown lands under ALRA. The council's claim was denied, in part, because the land was considered inalienable, due to the National Park designation. Anangu persisted with their claim for Uluru, and in 1983 Northern Territory offered a perpetual lease or Territory free-hold, under the condition that no further claims be filed. The Anangu declined the offer. At the same time, Northern Territory proposed amendments to ALRA to restrict claims and prevent pastoral leases. The Commonwealth denied their proposal (Central Land Council 2003).

Tensions began to flare, and representatives for Northern Territory were bit-ter that their power over the park was diminishing and argued that Anangu were not a "real aboriginal community, but the creation of manipulative White activists" (Carruthers 2003:246). When Northern Territory received notice that the leaseback would be approved, a huge political storm erupted. The Coun-try Liberal Party and the Australian public vehemently opposed the return of Uluru–Kata Tjuta to Anangu owners and considered it a threat to tourism and the Northern Territory's economy. Northern Territory government representa-tives were active in these protests.

The negotiations that led to the leaseback of Uluru–Kata Tjuta illustrate the larger debates in Australia over Indigenous land claims, significance of sacred sites, and the challenge to Australian identity. National opinion was divided. Al-though some Australians viewed the return as helping to bridge differences be-tween Aboriginal and white Australians, the federal Labor government and others viewed the leaseback as a dangerous precedent. The Australian National opinion poll undertaken in 1985 advised that Ayers Rock had "emerged as one of the most powerful symbols against land rights. It is seen as an important part of Australia which should belong to all Australians. The granting of Ayers Rock to the Aborigi-nal people symbolises all the fears—'sacred sites everywhere'; refusal of public entry; 'land grabs'; giving away 'precious land'" (quoted in Hueneke 2006:34).

Despite these protests, in 1985 the Commonwealth amended ALRA and re-turned Uluru–Kata Tjuta National Park to the Uluru–Kata Tjuta Aboriginal Land Trust, a group composed of traditional park owners, with the understanding that the owners would *immediately* lease Uluru to the director of National Parks and Wildlife Service for a period of 99 years (Uluru–Kata Tjuta Board of Manage-ment/ANPWS 2000:9, emphasis mine). The memorandum of lease, lodged at the Registrar General's office for Northern Territory, indicates that the term of lease runs through October 25, 2084. The lands surrounding Uluru–Kata Tjuta are un-der aboriginal freehold title and held by the Petermann and Katiti Land Trusts.

Two points in the original lease were renegotiated in the final hours: the lease was extended from fifty to ninety-nine years, and climbing was permitted on Uluru. In 1986 the park terminated the working relationship with Northern

Territory because the heated opposition had created a situation where working relations had "become untenable" (Uluru–Kata Tjuta Board of Management/ ANPWS 2009:14).

Park Management Today

The 1999 Environment Protection and Biodiversity Conservation (EPBC) Act provides the legal framework for the management of the park. Although the Traditional Owners and Parks Australia share decision-making for the management of the park, final decisions rest with the director of National Parks Australia. Under the act, the director administers, manages, and is directed to protect the interests of the Traditional Owners. Parks Australia follows the definition of National Parks and Protected Areas required under the EPBC Act and established by the International Union for Conservation and Nature (IUCN), one of the primary advisers for World Heritage cultural landscapes. Uluru–Kata Tjuta National Park is assigned in IUCN Category II, a natural area of land or sea, and managed mainly for ecosystem protection and recreation. Although Parks Australia recognizes the importance of Traditional Owners in managing lands, they are obligated to protect the natural, scenic, and international significance of the sites.[2]

Joint management is a consensus-based approach to resource management. In 1979, Kakadu National Park became the first co-managed national park in Australia, the result of many years of negotiations between Traditional Owners and the Australian government (see De Lacy 1994). The Mirrar feared that the Commonwealth and Northern Territory mismanaged their lands by issuing mining exploration licenses to companies to extract uranium. They were outraged at the destructive land-use practices and mobilized the park's status as a World Heritage site to protect their lands. The Traditional Owners "broke the normal UNESCO protocols" and contacted the World Heritage Committee to have the park placed on the World Heritage in Danger list (Logan 2007:48). Members of Australia ICOMOS (International Council on Monuments and Sites), the national advisory body to UNESCO, were frustrated over the breach of protocol.

The 2009–19 Draft Management Plan described the process of joint management as collaborative and bringing together cultural and scientific knowledge as a way to interpret and manage the landscape. The lease requires a working relationship between managers and Traditional Owners and the understanding that the philosophy of Tjukurpa, or Anangu Law, defines and governs all aspects of activities; managers are required to respect these rules. This includes ensuring that Anangu can maintain their relationships to sacred places and protect the integrity of their Country. In this light, management policies identify sacred sites, and Tjukurpa tracks to prevent violations. In exchange, Parks Australia representatives agreed to maintain an Aṉangu majority on the Board of Management and encourage maintenance of Aṉangu traditions.

Plans of Management

The Uluṟu–Kata Tjuṯa Board of Management and Parks Australia prepare a Plan of Management every seven years. There is a strong, if at times implicit, focus on the natural heritage values of the park. The adoption of an IUCN category is consistent with Parks Australia's promotion of natural heritage resources. Park managers are charged protecting the natural and ecological values of the park in its "natural state" in ways that ensure ecological stability. The park's natural heritage resources are equated with aesthetic considerations, and activities that conserve and protect natural resources, such as wild plants and animals, are prioritized. The focus on these values promotes the park's landscapes as having inherent scientific, aesthetic, and conservation value. It is clear that Uluṟu and Kata Tjuṯa contain impressive natural features, habitats, and ecosystems. Aṉangu, however, view the natural and cultural values of the park within a different framework, and their understandings emphasize their connection and responsibilities to Country. Moreover, the "needs" of the Traditional Owners are considered as long as these do not conflict with park principles.

There is something lost in the translation from Western ideas of landscapes to Indigenous relationships to Country. Although Aṉangu's "aspirations" are considered by managers, they must also promote their natural and recreational values. Tjukurpa is used as a way to understand Aṉangu's relationship to the ecological and geological resources in the park. Yet, this interpretation of this relationship flattens out the complexities of Tjukurpa. The park discourse equates Aṉangu's spiritual values with the "symbolic embodiment of the Australian landscape." Although Aṉangu connect Tjukurpa with what are often identified as natural resources, this is not how Aṉangu interpret this connection.

The most recent plan now includes a well-developed section covering the concept of Indigenous Cultural and Intellectual Property (ICIP). The 2000 plan discussed ICIP briefly, in relation to the potential of bioprospecting. Although the Plan listed the ways managers will address how ICIP is used and controlled, Aṉangu are concerned with protecting ICIP. The plan noted that Aṉangu could copyright certain ICIP, though it also states that there are no laws to protect ICIP. This could be a problem as the Australian government, Northern Territory, and Parks Australia's shift to support exploration of the economic incentives of bioprospecting. Traditional ecological knowledge (TEK) or Indigenous knowledge (IK) has become central to engaging with descendant communities when managing Australian landscapes. The Uluru Fauna Survey is one example of managers attempting to collect and incorporate these approaches in park initiatives. In 1993, managers hired ecologists, botanists, and geographers to work with Anangu and collect TEK of vertebrates and the environment. One report noted that scientists' theories about landscapes differed significantly from Anangu beliefs (Reid et al. 1993). This likely relates to project design and the fact that it was conducted by scientists interested in natural resources and conserving fauna.

One challenge for joint management is that some practices and knowledge of Tjukurpa, such as burning and gathering practices, are seen in ecological terms. At the same time, it is true that many current management strategies have evolved to reflect shifting attitudes toward the environment. While earlier management strategies focused on surveying natural resources, today these foci have shifted to include traditional management practices, including fire. Fire management is central to Anangu's care for Country (Kohen 2003:231). They use fire to protect arid environments, manage flora and fauna, and mark life passages. Only those who have the rights and the detailed knowledge to burn can use fire. Although fire regimes within the park are largely seen as beneficial, some believe that burning is detrimental to nutrient cycling, slower-reproducing plant species, and some small mammals that need a longer fire-free period. Although managers may be correct in their assessments of potential impacts, fire management might also be seen as beneficial. Park managers cited fire management to illustrate the cultural heritage values of the park to the World Heritage Committee.

Perhaps the most contentious issue is climbing. The Traditional Owners do not condone climbing the Uluru monolith. Uluru is sacred and accessible only to initiated Mala men (Findley 2005:92). Anangu believe that climbing is in clear violation of Tjukurpa. Moreover, many people have died climbing Uluru, and Anangu, as custodians of the climb, are responsible. In the absence of clear guidelines and prohibitions for climbing, over 150,000 visitors each year choose to climb, despite efforts by Anangu to educate visitors about cultural disruptions. Following a campaign to educate visitors, the number of visitors who climb has decreased.

In a surprise shift, Parks Australia announced in 2009 that it was working toward closing the climb. In 2010 the park board proposed to close the climb if the numbers of climbers fell below 20 percent of the number of annual visitors.[3] As of this publication, despite the numbers falling below 20 percent, the park has not yet closed the climb. When the park announced the closure, members of Northern Territory's tourism board and the general public immediately op-posed the proposal. Prime Minister Kevin Rudd argued against the ban, stating that "as a matter of general principle my view has always been that people should be able to have appropriate access to Uluru."[4] Northern Territory's tourism min-ister, Chris Burns, agreed, arguing that Northern Territory has "never supported the full closure of the climb at Uluru and that remains our position."[5] Tourism Australia denounced the ban.

The opposition to the climbing ban mirrors demonstrations and protests in the 1980s that challenged the leaseback of the park to the Traditional Owners. Anangu, once again, are forced to defend their position against non-Indigenous groups who consider Uluru part of their national identity. This, of course, relates back to the narratives of the Australian outback that define Australia's nation-alist mythology (see, e.g., du Cros and Johnston 2002). Those who oppose the climb may be trying to protect their connection to Australian identity. To many non-Indigenous Australians, climbing is tied to their sense of connection to the landscape. Climbing Uluru is enmeshed in larger social, economic, politi-cal, and cultural struggles between competing stakeholders. The new develop-ment in policy may point to productive changes. Another way to think about the climbing issue at the park is how it is framed around control of a political resource. By returning control of the monolith back to the Anangu community, the park would establish that it is working toward addressing the unequal power relations that exist, and in the process it would legitimize the Anangu's respon-sibilities to Uluru. Nevertheless, it took twenty-five years to initiate this change, and it has not happened yet. Still, a potential change in policy is significant and an important step in recognizing Indigenous rights.

Areas of concern are constantly evolving; bioprospecting, a controversial and complex practice that applies traditional knowledge and resources to de-velop commercial interests, has been identified as a potential revenue source. The park considers bioprospecting a "high priority." Bioprospecting is often promoted as a way to preserve biodiversity and Indigenous knowledge, but it is more often used for commercial, pharmaceutical, agricultural, industrial, and chemical applications (see Hayden 2003). Bioprospecting falls under the framework of the Environment Protection Act, and any potential development or project in the park would require an environmental impact assessment. Because the director is responsible under the lease for the maintenance and enhancement of the park and its values, he or she would be the primary spokes-person and decision maker for these matters. Although bioprospecting has not occurred on any significant level, the park recommends that Anangu consider bioprospecting as an option for economic gain (Uluru–Kata Tjuta Board of Management/ANPWS 2009:119).

Bioprospecting falls within the larger debates over Indigenous claims to intellectual and cultural property knowledge being used for commercial interests (see Greene 2004; Hayden 2003). Appropriation and misuse of traditional knowledge for commercial interests could be detrimental for future control over ICIP. It is unclear how profits affect Indigenous rights or access. Park managers will need to work with Anangu to consider if bioprospecting interferes with ICIP or Tjukurpa. The Commonwealth considers bioprospecting non-invasive, though I would argue that it could be in conflict with Tjukurpa. It is critical that bioprospecting activities be agreed on by Anangu, as the park could establish a dangerous precedent that would allow the extraction or promotion of traditional plants or knowledge to be used for commercial interests.

Today, Anangu are placed in a paradoxical position of trying to negotiate how to protect Country while it is promoted as a major tourist destination (Griffin 2002:371). Anangu cite climbing, visual intrusion, vehicle traffic, soil erosion, overcrowding, and aircraft noise as violations of their traditional law. Park administrators are challenged to both support the park as a visitor attraction and protect Country. Although the plan emphasizes that Tjukurpa should be recognized by visitors, it does not always address violations of Anangu Law. The Uluru monolith is an iconic site and with the listing as a World Heritage site, the park has seen a marked increase in international visitors. Anangu ask that visitors do not access or take photographs of sacred sites, though these requests are often ignored. It is not clear how Anangu can protect the park when it is heavily promoted.

The struggle for land rights and the leaseback of the park reveal the larger social and historical context of these struggles. Differences in worldviews and relationships to Uluru–Kata Tjuta are at the heart of these negotiations. It is not that managers and government representatives do not understand the spiritual significance of Uluru–Kata Tjuta, but that they must work within a bureaucratic structure and framework that constrains understandings of Country. Anangu must make claims for their lands, resources, and intellectual property within a legal structure and system that privileges Western concepts of land and resources that in many ways are incompatible with their worldviews. Nevertheless, the leaseback in 1985 and the recent shift in park management policies related to the climb are steps toward acknowledging Anangu interests. Additionally, joint management of the park provides an opportunity to mediate current relationships between a Western scientific land-management system and that of the Anangu. What should not be overlooked is that joint management of the park is important to Anangu and was a strategy used to protect their lands.

World Heritage and Uluru–Kata Tjuta National Park

In 1986 the Commonwealth nominated the park for World Heritage status as a joint natural and cultural heritage site. The nomination cited the massive geological landmasses and natural scenic grandeur along with the cultural importance of the park. In 1987 an IUCN representative visited and recommended the park to the list under natural heritage criteria (ii) and (iii). Although the site was nominated under both natural and cultural criteria, for reasons that are not revealed, the cultural heritage advisory body ICOMOS did not evaluate the property (IUCN 1987). By December of that year, the World Heritage Committee reviewed the nomination prepared by Parks Australia (UNESCO 1987:2–3). In reference to UNESCO World Heritage criteria, IUCN proposed that Uluru–Kata Tjuta was significant under criteria (ii), associated with ongoing geological processes, (iii) examples of exceptional natural beauty and an exceptional combination of natural and cultural elements, and (iv) associated with habitat for rare and endangered species. The committee selected criteria (ii) and (iii) and deferred on criterion (iv) stating that other parks in Australia had better examples of these features. The committee did not adopt the cultural criteria, for reasons that are unclear.

The Commonwealth renominated the park in 1994 as a cultural heritage site under criteria (v) and (vi) and as a cultural landscape. With reference to criterion (v), the park was considered an "an outstanding illustration of successful human adaptation over many millennia to the exigencies of a hostile arid environment, the integrity of which would be threatened by any change to the present management system based on the practices of its Traditional Owners."[6] The site was also found significant under criterion (vi), citing the "dramatic monoliths of Uluru and Kata Tjuta [as forming] an integral part of the traditional belief system of one of the oldest human societies in the world."[7] The nomination was prepared with the consent of the Mutitjulu Aboriginal community and cited the ongoing and evolving relationship between the Anangu and the park. The committee accepted the nomination at the eighteenth session of the World Heritage Committee, and Uluru–Kata Tjuta National Park became the second property to be listed under the cultural landscape designation in 1994.

I reviewed the nomination file for Uluru–Kata Tjuta, which includes documents, photographs, reports, and other materials such as notes and correspondence with National and International Committees, ICOMOS Scientific Committees, and other experts, such as archaeologists and landscape architects. My review revealed that there was a palpable split between natural and cultural heritage that relates to IUCN's philosophy. IUCN, for example, recommended removal of cultural heritage from their mandates and sought to amend the World Heritage Operational Guidelines. The 1987 IUCN nomination and technical evaluation summaries, data sheet, and site visit notes for the park emphasized ranking species and habitats and discussed the status of threatened, endangered, and other sensitive species. The report also devoted considerable space to explaining the ongoing geological processes and the "exceptional natural beauty and exceptional combination of natural and cultural elements" (IUCN 1987:4). The report promoted a conservation approach to the natural resources within the park and recommended standards for habitat monitoring. To my knowledge, IUCN representatives did not collaborate with the Anangu, managers, or other state or federal agencies or conservation organizations in the preparation of their reports. There were no site-specific inventories undertaken to provide a baseline of natural resources within the park, and the reports relied on previous flora and fauna surveys for their recommendations. IUCN (1987:11) cited restoration of animal populations and plant communities and threats to the integrity of the park, particularly in the face of range management (the effects of feral animals, fire regimes, and visitors), and recommended developing educational and teaching strategies for tourists.

What is most revealing is that the materials developed by IUCN do not address cultural heritage values. I found these presented separately, largely in discussions that, for example, noted that the "overlay of the Aboriginal occupation adds a fascinating cultural aspect to the site" (IUCN 1987:12). The IUCN report provided one paragraph on the cultural heritage of the park that relates back to the natural features and emphasized the importance of natural heritage conservation. IUCN representatives I spoke with recommended protecting natural resources from loss or damage, ensuring the preservation of natural habitats and ecosystems, and protecting the geological and physiographic features of the park. They were not concerned about the cultural heritage values, or how Country would be protected.

Much of this relates to how nominations are undertaken. In 1994, ICOMOS sent archaeologists whose report emphasized a scientific and archaeological understanding of the park. In this case, it is clear that the experts drew on their archaeological backgrounds to identify Aboriginal heritage and landscapes. As the report reveals, Country was framed as material resources. For example, the experts cited Anangu's fire regimes as a way to link the natural features and resources to human agents and to illustrate how "Aboriginal peoples" interact with their landscapes. They also assessed universal and ideological values and the "long-term relationship" between the Anangu and their ability to adapt to a "hostile environment" as evidence of the ongoing "association between people and the land." As this demonstrates, the experts are constrained not only by disciplinary background but also by the definitions available to them in World Heritage contexts. As I have argued elsewhere, the definition of cultural landscapes provided in the World Heritage Operational Guidelines is broad and emphasizes land-use practices, natural resources, and the natural values (Baird 2009).

In general, the report was broad in scope, and data-collection procedures and theoretical and methodological grounding were not clear. In thinking of how to remediate Indigenous peoples' concerns, what would have added to the study was foregrounding ethnographic evidence of the contemporary importance and/or evolving relationship of the cultural landscape to Anangu. As discussed, Tjukurpa is a complex philosophy that cannot be equated to ecological and natural resources. Tjukurpa is not grounded in Western terms, and translating Anangu ideas of landscape within a scientific and material framework subordinates how the site is imagined and contested in the present. Western ideas of place form the basis of this authority. The nominations do not acknowledge this.

Aboriginal and local groups protested the inclusion of the heritage landscapes on the World Heritage list. Letters of opposition also included input from Indigenous groups, tourist and mining industry groups, and government entities, such as the West Coast Municipal Region, among others. In general, the letters opposed increased tourism or access to sites, loss of resource rights or land rights, and potential environmental impacts. In an internal letter sent to the UNESCO director, one writer apologized and "regretted the lack of coherence in World Heritage matters and some insufficient professional work carried out by IUCN experts."[8] Yet, based on my analysis of the nomination files and comparison to the final reports, opposition to the inclusion on the World Heritage list is suppressed from expert reports or is not included for other reasons. To my knowledge, none of the letters of protest from local, Aboriginal, or governmental groups were referenced in the site mission or final reports submitted to the World Heritage Committee.

It All Depends on the Land

As this example is meant to show, whether explicit or not, the World Heritage status of Uluṟu–Kata Tjuṯa National Park and its designation as a cultural landscape have implications for Traditional Owners. Experts, advisory bodies, and the World Heritage Committee interpret Aṉangu's heritage and, whether intentionally or not, assign values and create meaning. That is because experts tend to view Aboriginal landscapes as analogous to natural and material heritage. As I expand on in chapter 3, much of this relates to disciplinary foci as well as constraints on how heritage is defined. Yet the implications are severe, and in not bringing in the cultural importance and centrality of Country, experts may inadvertently misapply or misinterpret Aboriginal Law and knowledge systems that are land based. In World Heritage contexts, this likely relates back to the lack of Indigenous representation as experts, advisers, or members of advisory bodies or as voting members of scientific committees and heritage managers (see Baird 2009). Although managers consulted with and involved Traditional Owners in many of the studies, they were often working in a secondary role.

Although understandings of cultural landscapes differ in several respects, heritage experts tend not to acknowledge the epistemological underpinnings of their studies. Much of this relates to advisory bodies and their representatives, who often have different goals and missions that lead to widely different results. The main advisory bodies to the World Heritage Committee, IUCN and ICOMOS, drew conceptual boundaries between Aṉangu's cultural and natural heritage and between tangible and intangible heritage to make the claim for the park as a cultural landscape. Interestingly, the shift to cultural landscapes expanded the inventory and created new typologies and constructions of place. Aṉangu, however, were constrained to make their heritage fit within existing definitions and had to pluck out parts of it to stand for the whole.

The definition of cultural landscapes used by Parks Australia and the World Heritage Committee is problematic. To connect Aṉangu's Law to the idea that a cultural landscape represents "the combined works of nature and of man" is in error. The foundation of the landscape paradigm originated in Enlightenment and European cultural thinking and only loosely translates to the fine-grained and complex understanding of Uluṟu–Kata Tjuṯa by the Traditional Owners. Why does this matter? Because experts applied Western notions of landscapes that worked in ways that renamed and reconceptualized Aṉangu's relationship to Country. That is, they promoted the cultural and natural heritage resources and values. Similar to early explorers who renamed the geographies of Uluṟu–Kata Tjuṯa, the interpretation of Aṉangu's Country as a cultural landscape places Indigenous stakeholders in the same position: they must defend and explain their rights to Country. They must also define their heritage within intellectual and bureaucratic structures that tend to subjugate and/or negate their views. The use of Country as a proxy or stand-in for cultural landscapes misrepresents the true meaning, flattens the complexity of the association, and overlooks the Aṉangu's custodial and spiritual responsibilities to place.

The Parks and World Heritage advisory bodies do not present competing meanings of the landscape and thus restrict alternative interpretations. This is where some of the problems lie. Experts involved in the nominations typically spend a few days or a week at the nominated site and rely on information submitted by the nominating Country, whose goal is to increase the number of World Heritage properties. In the case of the park, the site nomination originated from scientists and scholars primarily interested in collecting scientific data about the natural resources and environments in the park, not from Aṉangu. Integration of Aṉangu-centered understandings of place and their participation in deciding what actually constitutes a cultural landscape, or more appropriately, an Aboriginal landscape, could have helped to address this disparity. It is my assertion that much of this relates back to the colonial legacies and histories of dispossession that have worked against Indigenous participation in heritage outcomes.

The discourses of natural heritage values, knowledge, and relationships legitimize the natural heritage values and resources of the park. The definitions that IUCN applied to understand heritage promoted the management of habitats and natural resources and only *added* the cultural heritage values as an aside. As Laurajane Smith (2004:195) has argued, the management of heritage is ultimately the "management and governance of the meanings and values that the material heritage is seen to symbolize or otherwise represent." The irony here is that the cultural landscape designation was created, in part, to redress changes in IUCN definitions of cultural landscapes that privileged natural heritage. Uluṟu–Kata Tjuṯa heritage managers shifted their definitions to match what they wanted to protect or promote. While earlier management plans directed by IUCN promoted the natural heritage values and resources, they suppressed the cultural heritage values of the park. Because the park was not accepted as a cultural heritage site, representatives tried again and used the cultural landscape designation as a way to have the cultural heritage values recognized. This also means that Indigenous groups could use this designation to mediate the disproportionate focus on natural heritage values that erase or devalue their understanding of place. However, cultural landscapes, as defined by the World Heritage Committee, do not yet adequately reflect Indigenous understandings of place.

To be clear, heritage scholars, experts, and managers *do* work hard to recognize Aboriginal rights and resources. Members of ICOMOS Australia, for example, lobbied to prohibit climbing. With increases in visitors seeking to climb and tour companies that promote climbing, their support is crucial to protecting Tjukurpa. Nevertheless, ancient landscapes and natural monuments are often embraced by settler nations as a way to create a sense of historical connection. This is obviously at play at Uluru–Kata Tjuta. The park is now on an international stage and attracts outsiders who want to connect with and explore Indigenous culture and lands.[9] What has not yet been explored is how heritage landscapes evoke these connections. That Anangu's Country is to be shared is something that will need to be thought through. Anangu do not share knowledge with everyone, and the park's World Heritage status could contribute to the abuse of their knowledge. The distribution of local knowledge in international contexts has not been addressed. Nevertheless, the cultural landscape designation *has* helped land managers address the disproportionate focus on the park's natural heritage values. The inclusion of cultural heritage values provides a venue to address issues that previously caused discord and new directions for land managers and Anangu to collaborate. Nonetheless, managers will have to tread lightly as cultural landscapes are often loosely defined in heritage contexts, which may have implications for how sites are managed.

The joint management of Uluru–Kata Tjuta by Parks Australia and the Traditional Owners has been promoted as a collaborative contract and relationship. While this may be true, at the same time one must consider that largely absent from the park and World Heritage documents, policies, mandates, recommendations, and research is the colonial history from which the park was formed. Erased in the process are the historical, social, and political contexts related to Anangu's land claims: the history of conflict, the jockeying by the Commonwealth and Northern Territories for power, and the social conditions that led to the Anangu's fight for their Country. The leaseback and joint management framework for the park were results of the Traditional Owners' struggles to reclaim their lands and to maintain their custodial responsibilities required under their Aboriginal Law. These contexts, however uncomfortable, should be part of the discussion.

Perhaps most problematic is how the histories of dispossession and loss are occluded in park narratives. It is not that these histories are not known, but instead that a narrative of collaboration and goodwill replaces it. Such omissions prevent a more complex account of hegemonic practices and policies. Some may say that the joint management of the park is evidence of shared power structure between managers and Traditional Owners. But this occludes the real power that exists in these negotiations. In the case of the leaseback, although the struggles for the leaseback are discussed, they are largely removed from the context of colonialism and later sovereignty and land struggles. Where are the histories of dispossession and assimilation? This conservative and occluded narrative collapses history and prevents discussions between Aṉangu and others who challenge their claim to these lands. Aṉangu's version of these histories is not included in park narratives. The failure to grapple with this history undermines their authority in land claims and their evolving relationship to Uluṟu–Kata Tjuṯa. National parks, as Carruthers (2003:244) stated, are "divisive institutions where meanings of land and space collide, and this assertion holds true for Uluṟu–Kata Tjuṯa." Although Aṉangu are presented as equal partners in the management of cultural landscapes, in many cases their needs were ignored if they came in conflict with the park's mission. Despite their position as owners and joint managers of the park, they do not have full control of how their heritage is represented. Aṉangu agreed, in part, to the joint management, because it was the best strategy to address an asymmetrical relationship and reclaim a voice in how their lands were managed.

At the same time, we must be mindful how the discourses of heritage privilege science, material culture, and tangible heritage. The idea that Indigenous notions of ecology and natural resources are compatible with science has been acknowledged before (Berkes 1999; Pretty et al. 2009). What is not often discussed is how these different knowledge systems are often not congruent. Although scientists and Aṉangu have collaborated and produced valuable work, there are limits to the applicability of these studies for understanding cultural landscapes. What should be addressed, and is increasingly urgent, are the research designs and products of research in the park. Heritage experts, as knowledge producers and decision makers, do not always recognize that the knowledge they produce is used in other contexts. With the increased lobbying by corporations and the perceived investment in bioprospecting, it is possible that scientific understandings of land resources and uses could be used against Aṉangu. How do these interfere with Aṉangu's custodial and spiritual responsibilities, or their knowledge and intellectual practices?

We must be cognizant that nomination and placement on the World Heritage list is also part of a larger nation-building enterprise. As such, the representation of the park is not neutral; it creates a particular set of meanings that have legibility beyond their local context. But perhaps the omissions can also be attributed to how such sociopolitical contexts are occluded in most heritage negotiations. The question is how these constructions of heritage serve to empower some while simultaneously alienating others. Can Aṉangu afford to have their cultural heritage on display for an international audience? Clearly, there are wider implications of heritage practices and consequences for Indigenous peoples' claims to land, resources, and political authority.

3

Of Environments and Landscapes

It would be hard to imagine a worse place for an oil spill.

Ecologist John Wiens describing the Exxon Valdez spill

Kosciusko Island, Southeast Alaska, August 2004

In the summer of 2004, I traveled to Kosciusko Island located off the shore of Prince of Wales Island in Alaska, in the traditional territories of the Heinya kwaan and Takjik'aan kwaan Tlingit people (see Map 2). I was invited to join the Kosciusko Island Rock Art Project, sponsored by Tongass National Forest and part of a newly envisioned Heritage Expedition—a way to undertake cultural resource fieldwork and draw on ecotourism support.[1] Tongass had been described to me as one of Alaska's wildest landscapes, and I was excited to have an opportunity to visit the region. On my flight to the island, my mood shifted from excitement to despair as I watched the thick canopy of temperate rain forest give way to vast timber clear-cuts and entire mountaintops denuded of trees.[2] Driving over Prince of Wales Island was equally disturbing: heavy rains had washed soils down slopes, and mile upon mile of slash piles and heavy undergrowth dominated most views. I could not help wondering how such seemingly destructive logging practices affected the health of these vital forest systems, the watershed and the soils, as well as the habitats of forest-dependent animals. When I shared my concerns with others on the trip, including a member of the Sealaska Heritage Institute, I was taken aback when she enthusiastically supported logging on the island.[3] From my naive perspective, I had mistakenly equated Native peoples' interests with conservation approaches.

My understanding of Tongass National Forest now encompasses a broader view, one that sees it as both a social and a contested landscape. The forest includes a complicated patchwork of federal, state, Native, and private lands. Stakeholders include land-management agencies, industry representatives, Alaska Native groups, scientists, locals, and environmental NGOs, each with a different approach to conservation, connections to place, and ideas of what

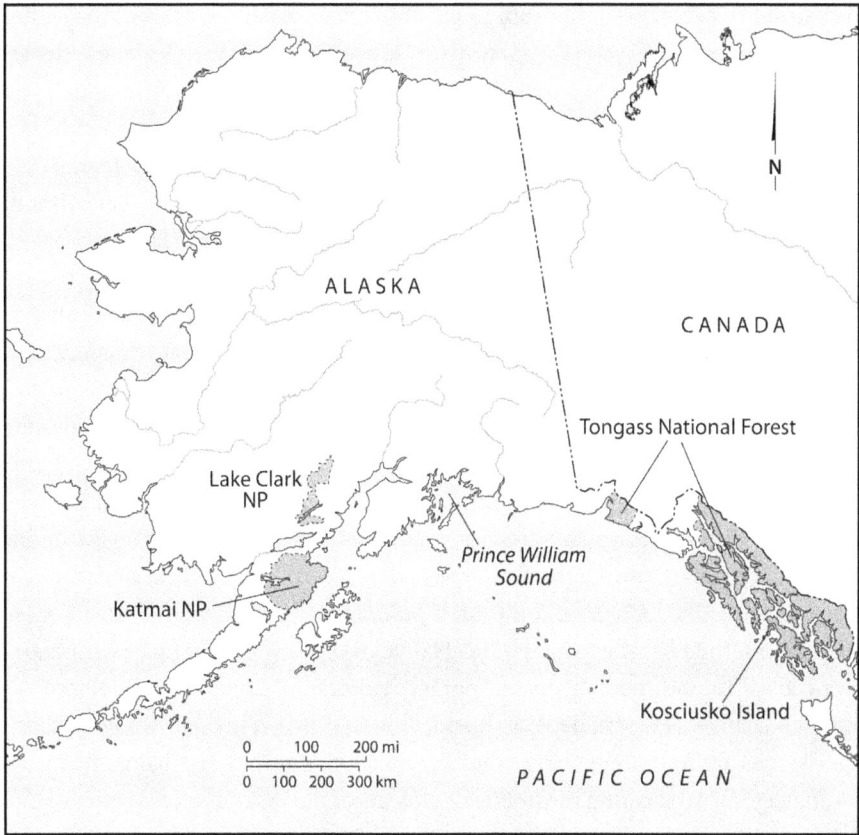

Map 2. Alaska with principal field sites, map by Bill Nelson.

constitutes environmental impacts. Natural resource policy expert Martin Nie (2006:386) has described Tongass as "perhaps the most controversial national forest in the country." Although stakeholders today have collaborated to assess climate-change vulnerability and define its social, ecological, and economic costs, at the time of our project, forest managers, private industry actors, and legislators were engaged in protracted debates over forest management initiatives and practices and timber quotas (see, e.g., Beier et al. 2009; Durbin 2005).[4] Yet, our project existed in isolation of these larger contexts.[5] But if you consider federal legislation passed in 2014 now provides seventy thousand acres of the forest to Sealaska to log, including a large area of Kosciusko Island, then the project takes on a different hue. Some have even charged Sealaska with circumventing environmental laws and regulations and masking unsustainable logging practices within terms of Indigenous rights to resources (Dombrowski 2002).

Whatever the case, it is important to position heritage landscapes within a wider frame. Viewing the project in this way would require understanding the histories of individuals, institutions, and agencies adapting to changes in the political, cultural, and economic landscape as well as how competing interests from industry, tourism, public land needs, and a regional boom-and-bust economy intersect.

Ignoring the forest politics comes at a cost. Over the course of my fieldwork in Kosciusko, I came to realize that our engagement with heritage landscapes (i.e., management, interpretation, conservation) requires more than an inventory, description, or analysis of its cultural or natural resources. It requires attending to the complicated (and often occluded) histories and contemporary frictions and tensions. If we know that forests (or landscapes) are "deeply cultural and political" (Braun 2002:8), then how do we position them within a wider frame, with an acute attentiveness to their sociopolitical entanglements and historical antecedents? This chapter explores this question, looking specifically at contexts related to heritage landscapes intersecting with human-caused disasters and climate-change/sustainability initiatives. Drawing from two research projects—the cultural landscapes of the central Gulf of Alaska and the Altai Mountains of Mongolia—I situate these sites within their broader sociopolitical contexts to show how heritage landscapes are central to and mediate contemporary debates on sustainable development, climate change, resource depletion, and disasters. As I argue here, how heritage landscapes are interpreted have consequences for how they are maintained and/or managed. Not locating the political contexts of our work has consequences.[6]

The "Human Spill": Prince William Sound, Alaska

Located in the north Gulf of Alaska, Prince William Sound includes an intricate system of bays, fjords, inlets, and islands (see Map 2.).[7] The Sound includes over two thousand miles of shoreline and provides a mosaic of freshwater, marine, and terrestrial habitats for fish, birds, shellfish, and terrestrial and marine mammals. Archaeological and oral historical evidence reflect at least four thousand years of use and complex interactions with cultures throughout the North Pacific Region (Crowell and Mann 1998; Reger 1998). By the late 1700s, Russian and English explorers, fur hunters, and missionaries made their way to the region, and by the late nineteenth century these explorers established mines, commercial fisheries, canneries, and timber mills (Wooley 1995). Despite the influx of industry and immigrants, Alaska Native groups have maintained a strong cultural and spiritual connection to the Sound.

The Sound is a dynamic landscape. In 1964, Prince William Sound was the epicenter for the Good Friday Earthquake, an extreme earthquake (magnitude 9.2) that transformed the topography through uplift, landslides, and tsunamis. The region was also the epicenter for the 1989 *Exxon Valdez* oil spill, which, until the *Deepwater Horizon* spill in the Gulf of Mexico in 2010, was the largest oil spill in the United States. Due to a series of factors, including pilot error (alcohol and lack of sleep) and inexperience, the *Exxon Valdez* grounded on Bligh Reef and spilled nearly 11 million gallons of toxic crude oil. Disaster responders could not immediately contain the spill, and severe storms, high winds, and the North Pacific and Alaska currents distributed the crude oil to nearly thirteen hundred miles of shoreline (Hanable and Burkhart 1990). Hundreds of thousands of animals were killed and many, many more injured. The crude oil contaminated the "food chain beginning with plankton and continuing through the oiled carcasses of its victims" (Hanable and Burkhart 1990:9). Commercial fisheries and tourist industries closed and, communities struggled with the social, economic, and environmental impacts of the disaster, the legacies of which are still felt deeply today. Despite enormous efforts to assess the recovery of the Sound's ecosystems, the long-term impacts of this event are still debated (see, e.g., Mobley 1990; Wiens 2013).

The spill severely disrupted Alaska Native communities' subsistence economies and practices and caused a profound cultural loss (after Kirsch 2001). Communities struggled with the loss of marine and terrestrial plants and animal resources, and efforts to minister to the damage to traditional and sacred sites were often stymied by larger environmental cleanup efforts. The significance of these social, cultural, environmental, and psychological impacts were often overlooked and cleanup efforts often intensified disruptions (Gill 1997). It is beyond the scope of this discussion to expand on the damage and devastation of this catastrophic human-caused event. Instead, I focus here on the role of conservation specialists, heritage managers, and scientists in the post-spill recovery efforts.

The *Exxon Valdez* oil spill was not only an environmental disaster; it was also a cultural phenomenon, what Morrison (1993:432) aptly coined the "human spill."[8] The spill "became the most intensively studied oil spill in history" (Wiens 2013:xxii). Thousands of people—disaster responders, cleanup workers, academics, scientists, contractors, industry representatives, and media—came to assist in the cleanup effort. Directed by the U.S. Coast Guard in consultation with Exxon, state agencies, and contractors, these efforts included more than eleven thousand people and at least a thousand boats (Wiens 2013:13; see also O. R. Harrison 1991). Despite Alaska Natives' participation in the cleanup efforts, many found the intrusion of people as disruptive as the spill itself. Well-meaning responders, for example, unknowingly disturbed cultural sites and plants and animals. And what was not widely shared or known was that the spill occurred "at the peak of the preparation phase of their subsistence cycle" (Gill 1997:169). The Alaska Native community members I have spoken with have repeatedly stated that subsistence harvesting, hunting, and sharing are essential to cultural continuity and are important traditions that unite their communities.

Although cultural resources were clearly a concern, the majority of the recovery, assessment, and monitoring projects focused on ecological and environmental impacts. These projects were part of the second wave of efforts that were funded through the *Exxon Valdez* Oil Spill Trustee Council, formed using funds from the $900 million civic settlement with the U.S. federal and Alaska governments.[9] The council supported restoration efforts, scientific studies, and research to record the legacies of the spill on ecosystems, water chemistry, shoreline ecology, fish and wildlife, animal and conservation rehabilitation, and, to a lesser extent, cultural resources (see, e.g., Wells et al. 1995; Wiens 2013).[10] Studies included analyses of the impacts of hydrocarbons in marine sediments, water quality on fish and crustaceans, and salmon and egg incubation and fry survival. Similarly, federal, state, and local agencies undertook research, some of which reported contradictory results (see Wiens 2013:xxii). Together these studies comprise more than twenty thousand documents, two thousand scientific reports, as well as books, technical reports, theses, dissertations, and conference presentations (see Johnson and Rustin 2013:xx).

It is important to recognize that agencies debated whether archaeological heritage was considered a resource within the scope of spill cleanup and governance. As archaeologist Doug Reger and his colleagues (2000:1) lamented, a "coordinated agency assessment did not begin until two years after the spill." In other words, cultural resources were not a top priority in recovery efforts. There were differing legal opinions and scopes of interest related to agencies' mandates as well as competing ideas of just exactly where cultural resources fit within cleanup activities. In the end, cultural resources were seen as falling under Section 106 of the National Historic Preservation Act, in part due to the efforts of the U.S. Coast Guard, which pushed to include impacts to archaeological sites within recovery and cleanup efforts. Nevertheless, impacts to cultural resources were a concern to many cultural resource managers and agencies, and the *Exxon Valdez* Cultural Resource Program was created to address damages to cultural resources, and to comply with federal and state laws.[11] An unprecedented number of archaeological surveys were conducted, and archaeologists inventoried cultural sites throughout the spill area (Mobley 1990). The program also supported longitudinal studies to monitor impacts and collect materials and sediment samples found in oiled sites, and included areas in Alaska Peninsula, Kodiak Archipelago, and the coastal regions of Outer Cook Inlet and the Kenai Peninsula (see, e.g., Jesperson and Griffin 1992; Mobley 1990; Reger et al. 2000:1).

Not surprisingly, the impacts of the oil spill on biodiversity and ecosystems, analyses of restoration efforts and water quality, and other environmental issues have remained the primary concern of the recovery efforts (see, e.g., Wells et al. 1995; Wiens 2013). To be sure, understanding the recovery of ecological communities is essential. Be that as it may, I suggest that although these insights are enormously important, the separation of cultural and natural resources has had unintended consequences. The best way to ensure the health and longevity of the Sound is to include a holistic understanding of the entirety of the region. At this time, our studies do not provide a way to do this.

Of Orcas and Otters

Some fifteen years after the *Exxon Valdez* oil spill, on an overcast afternoon in June, I climbed onboard the *Auklet,* a sixty-foot vessel owned by a local captain and his wife (see Figure 2). The crew also included a Forest Service archaeologist and a rock-art photographer. Our mission: to visit rock art and archaeological sites throughout Prince William Sound. We knew we had a busy field research trip ahead and were excited to finally be onboard. I had known that the recovery of many species in the Sound had been slow, and we were heartened to see a pod of orcas swimming alongside the *Auklet* as we neared the southern end of Hinchinbrook Island in Orca Bay.

A bit of background on the project will be useful here. In 2003, I completed a research project for Lake Clark National Park and Preserve in which I analyzed archaeological materials and pictographs at two sites, Tuxedni Bay and Clam Cove (Baird 2003). I was following the work of anthropologist Frederica de Laguna, who in the 1930s surveyed coastal archaeological sites throughout Cook Inlet and Prince William Sound. De Laguna's pioneering work generated considerable archaeological and ethnographic data and inspired subsequent studies of these regions (e.g., Workman 1998; Yarborough 2000). Her study of the precontact pictographs found in these regions (de Laguna 1934, 1956) was less frequently discussed. In 2002, I met with Dr. de Laguna to discuss my work in Lake Clark, her survey of pictograph sites in outer Cook Inlet, and her opinion about relationships between the Cook Inlet and Prince William Sound pictographs. She stood by her earlier hypothesis that the pictographs of the Sound "find their closest analogy in the Eskimo pictographs of Cook Inlet" (de Laguna 1956:109) and encouraged me to analyze the imagery of these two regions more closely.

I contacted the forest archaeologist for the Chugach National Forest and proposed that we undertake a joint project to compare what we knew of the outer Cook Inlet pictographs with new data from sites located throughout the Sound. I was keen to expand the project to include analyses of Prince William Sound as

Figure 2. Fieldwork in Prince William Sound, Alaska, photo by Carolynne Merrill.

a cultural landscape and to conduct ethnographic interviews with Chugach representatives about the contemporary sociopolitical significance of the sites. The Forest Service supported the project and expanded the scope to include visiting sites that were at risk and part of the Archaeological Index Site Monitoring project, a project funded to monitor vandalism and other impacts on archaeological sites after the *Exxon Valdez* oil spill in 1989 (see Reger et al. 2000).

While in the field, I became increasingly distracted and had to remind myself that I was there to focus on the region's archaeology—not its history and politics or the *Exxon Valdez* oil spill. And although the research data that we collected provided insights into ideas of culture areas, I was preoccupied with a very different set of questions: Why do we not include the sociopolitical contexts in our reports and in our sharing of our research? When I review my notes and reflect back, I realize that I was struggling to think of ways to include these concerns. Specifically, I was challenged to reconcile the work I was doing with the reality of the long-lasting impacts of the spill. My focus on cultural landscapes and the nature of past human occupation of the region and the significance within the larger archaeological, ethnographic, and regional context did not provide a clear venue or opportunity to discuss the lived, real, political, economic, and social contexts of the spill.

Although our first day in Prince William Sound seemed serendipitous in that we were greeted by orcas and northern sea otters, as we pressed on we encountered some troubling signs: lingering oil in nearshore habitats, remains of sea otter and unidentifiable animals and birds, and what appeared to be a recently looted archaeological sites. I could not prove that the remains were related to the spill, but when I compare these experiences to discussions I had with people who lived and worked in the region—that is, with Chugach representatives, Forest Service employees, scientists, locals, and fishermen—something revealing emerged. Nearly fifteen years after the spill, each group struggled with reconciling the impacts of the disaster. Although each shared a different experience, they continued to talk about the impact of the spill on their lives.

When I returned from the field, I began to analyze the data, work with the photographs, and transcribe my notes and interviews. I was still searching for a place to include those of my observations that were not related to the immediate project. Where does one include observations of the social and political contexts within an archaeological study of cultural landscapes? Is it appropriate, for example, to include statistics that show that the Chugach region reported a decrease of approximately 50 percent in subsistence hunting and gathering after the spill?[12] After such a profound experience in the field, in some ways my project felt quaint. I was analyzing the "cultural landscapes" through data collected on view sheds, place-names, material culture, and so on. Making matters worse, my Chugach interlocutor questioned how I conceptualized landscapes and noted that this was not how he thought of these places. To put it differently, my approach produced a fragmented, partial, and distorted image of the Sound.

For some time now, scholars of heritage have been raising concerns about the sociopolitical contexts of their work (see, e.g., Baird 2009; Weiss 2014). Scientists also discuss their challenges in reconciling their roles as objective observers with what they confront in the field. In her book *Into Great Silence*, the late marine biologist Eva Saulitis (2013) shared her struggles with reconciling expectations of being a scientist collecting data on the transient orcas in the Sound with the visceral realities of the spill. She also bristled at the implications and the constraints of receiving money from Exxon. It took time for her to share these experiences and the impacts of the spill on her work and life, and even then she was criticized for taking a political stance. As naturalist Barry Lopez (2001) wrote, an area "of particular discomfort for naturalists" is "how to manage emotional grief and moral indignation in pursuits so closely tied to science, with its historical claim to objectivity."

Some will argue that such separation of personal views and research is necessary to undertake "value-free" and "objective" research. But perhaps it may also be true that when we compartmentalize our knowledge and parse it out into separate and unconnected parts, we produce research that is incomplete and, dare I say, in error. These fragmentary approaches are built into *how* we present our work: none of the final products from my research in Prince William Sound included *any* discussion of the *Exxon Valdez* oil spill. Instead, these concerns remain silenced in my notes. When I discussed my concerns with a mentor, I was advised that I would need to reframe my project to take on these more "anthropological" concerns. In other words, my study of cultural landscapes would need to be abandoned.

What my ethnographic interviews and experiences in the field did show was that the sites we visited throughout the Sound had varied degrees of importance to local groups and descendant communities. As an illustration, one pictograph site in the Knight Island Passage shows these complexities. Ethnographically, we know that the site was home to the Palugvirmiut peoples, and my interview with my Chugach interlocutor indicated that this site today holds continued importance, though it is not visited because it is a burial site. The pictographs at the site include images of umiaks that can be seen from near-shore waters. In 1902, scientist Edmond Meany was reported to have removed seven mummies in full sea-hunting regalia from the rock shelter and sent these to the Smithsonian (Meany 1906), although a *New York Times* article contradicts this report. Instead, it is likely that prospectors had removed the human remains in hopes of receiving money. Nevertheless, this history of plunder ties into the larger fascination with collecting Indigenous peoples' remains and materials.

To tell the history of this site, one would need to include, for example, the history of Palugvirmiut peoples or early-twentieth-century fox farmers and miners who lived on the island. One would need to note the various archaeologists, geologists, environmental scientists, biologists, and oil spill responders who have visited and/or worked on the island. One would need to ask why Greek Orthodox crosses are used to mark contemporary burials. In thinking of the landscape as a sacred site, one would need to know its real name as well as its uses and meanings. What was the impact of contact and colonization, the maritime fur trade, or extractive activities on the island? One would also need to discuss the high-energy beach of the island, the site where Eva Saulitis's beloved orca, Eyak, a member of the AT1 group, was found in 2000. This group is a unique family of transient whales known only from this region, who lost eleven of twenty-two members in the three years after the *Exxon Valdez* spill (Saulitis 2013). To be clear, the significance and meaning of this site goes well beyond its archaeological or cultural history.

That is to say, if we rely on archaeological evidence or environmental data as the framework in which to describe such places, we miss the contemporary meanings and how people still interact with these sites today. How do we include the stories of the animals—the sea otters, birds, plankton, and seaweeds that perished in the spill? How do we talk of renewal and loss? As a cultural landscape, the Sound is only viewed one way, but viewing this area as a heritage landscape allows one to see this place with multiple, hybrid, and often-contradictory meanings, a landscape of transformation as much as one of loss and renewal, that is, a landscape inscribed and reinscribed with meaning. In the remainder of this chapter I turn to a different heritage landscape, the Mongolian Altai, to show how, like Prince William Sound, landscapes are central to contemporary sustainability and climate-change initiatives.

Climate Change and Heritage in the Mongolian Altai

Without a doubt, travel in northwestern Mongolia is not easy—roads etched into mountainsides, treacherous river crossings, unexpected thunderstorms and persistent winds—but the rewards far outweigh the risks: from snow-covered peaks and high-mountain valleys to standing stones that mark the confluence of sacred rivers, abundant birds and wildlife—demoiselle cranes, Siberian marmots, and Bactrian camels—and while I was there, a rumor of a sighting of the elusive and endangered snow leopard. Yet for all its beauty and grandeur, the Mongolian Altai, which shares its borders with Russia, China, and Kazakhstan, cannot escape the impacts of a warming planet (see Map 3). Local herders will tell you that the summers are hotter, the winters more extreme. Climate change here is not an abstraction, but instead a lived reality of pastures lost to wildfires, shrinking glaciers, declining water sources, smog masses and insect outbreaks.[13]

In 2006, I surveyed the high-mountain valleys of the Bayan Ölgiy province with a team that had been investigating the cultural landscapes of the region for many years. The cultural landscapes of the Altai are found in the extensive material culture spread across the region—standing stones and stone figures, stone altars, burial and ritual mounds, and petroglyphs that clearly are meant to evoke the geography of the place (see Figure 3). Archaeologists have dated these symbolic and cultural materials—found on high points and terraces, at the confluence of rivers, and on ancient trading routes—to at least twelve centuries years ago (Jacobson 1993). The project drew together data on archaeology and landscapes, and in the field we collected geospatial, photographic, and archaeological data as well as information on prominent landscape features, view sheds, and material culture. Although the exact meaning of how these places functioned as a "cultural landscape" cannot be known, we do know that different cultures marked the landscape in distinct ways. The Kazakh nomadic pastoralists, who live and move throughout its mountains and valleys today, are relatively recent migrants whose connection began only in the mid-1800s (Dubuisson and Genina 2011:478). Nevertheless, they too have an unmistakable connection to these landscapes. In the field I spoke informally with some of these local herders, who were concerned about the increased amount of

Map 3. Altai Mountains, northwestern Mongolia, map by Bill Nelson.

Figure 3. Standing stones, Bayan Ölgiy province, northwestern Mongolia, photo by Altai Survey Project, Ghent University.

people (scientists, prospectors, tourists and tour operators) who were imposing on their pastures and camping and traveling through the region.

The Altai region is perhaps best known, however, for the "frozen tombs" of the Scythian civilization from the Late Bronze and Early Iron Ages (ninth to third century B.C.), a culture originating in the Altai and ranging throughout the Eurasian steppe, from northern China to the Black Sea. Archaeologists have unearthed well-preserved tattooed human remains, sacrificial horses, wooden sarcophagi, gold vessels and ornaments, iron, and turquoise, preserved by permafrost that protects the organic materials (Bourgeois et al. 2007; Plets et al. 2011).[14] Material from these sites provides unique data that scientists have used to reconstruct the burial customs of these nomadic horse-riding cultures, from designs of animal or human figures on ornaments to the orientation of the burials, often with the inclusion of horses in full riding regalia that still have flesh, hair, and saddles intact. During our field season we visited an excavation by German archaeologists who had just unearthed one of these graves. We watched as archaeologists gingerly troweled sediments away from the find: a person buried in full regalia and with a coat lined with marmot and wool.[15] But with temperatures rising (and other climactic factors taking place), the permafrost is starting to thaw and archaeologists are rightly concerned. At the time of our survey the Altai region was under consideration for a UNESCO Transboundary Biosphere Reserve (TBR).[16] Archaeologists are active in discussions with national governments and international agencies to find ways to preserve these sites *in situ* (see Bourgeois et al. 2007).

Although being in the Altai helped me to think about "what people make of places," I also wondered how ideas of landscapes (or nature, wilderness, sustainability, and conservation, for that matter) interfered with or contradicted what these places mean to those who live there today (after Basso 1996). Throughout the season we came across evidence, albeit anecdotal, of environmental stresses: toxic smog masses, likely originating from China, water sources that had dried up, pastures that were denuded of grasses, feral animals, and areas overgrazed and overrun with insects. But we also encountered communities that were undergoing profound ethnic and social changes. In each of the small villages (called *aimags*) we visited on our fifteen-hundred-kilometer survey, we came across newly built mosques, indicating a resurgence and adherence to a particular faith. But these communities are also still grappling with the legacies of oppressive policies under sustained Soviet control and occupation that still affect Mongolian minorities and Indigenous Altain groups today. These communities were marginalized in the country's rebuilding efforts. Minority Rights Group International, for example, reported that ethnic minorities in the Bayan Ölgiy region are discriminated against based on race and ethnicity and that many members of the ethnic Kazakh groups face "widespread societal and institutional discrimination" (UNHRC 2011). Much like the Tongass National Forest example, the Mongolian Altai is deeply cultural and political and has complicated histories and contemporary frictions and tensions. Yet, similar to the Tongass example, the project existed in isolation of these larger sociopolitical, historical, and environmental contexts. What are these larger mediating contexts, and what is their impact on communities of the Altai?

With this question in mind, I attended the 2006 UNESCO-sponsored conference "The Cultural Landscape of the Altai Mountains," in Ghent, Belgium. The conference convened scientists and scholars active in heritage contexts, from promoting archaeological research to undertaking site visits and providing testimony to UNESCO and the International Union for Conservation and Nature (IUCN). As expected, most papers focused on issues related to the Scythian archaeology of the region, and in particular the threat to these archaeological sites related to climate change and permafrost melt that most assuredly would destroy organic materials. Scientists and scholars also convened to discuss the potential UNESCO nomination. Ironically, Mongolian officials were physically absent from the conference, as were the voices of the regional and local authorities, local communities, and the broader international mountain communities who would also be affected by the reserve and by World Heritage status. I spoke with conference participants and asked their opinion on the region and their conceptions of the landscapes. I found that few scholars conceptualized the Altai region as a cultural landscape, and few had explicitly addressed how nomadic herders or other communities would be affected by a World Heritage designation. To be clear, it is not that they were indifferent to local communities, as many have established long-term friendships with local communities, but instead that their work in the region related to examining the environmental and/or archaeological contexts.

The heritage landscapes of the Altai present an interesting case. To be sure, the impact of World Heritage status in this remote and environmentally vulnerable region is significant. Landscapes interpreted through the TBR follow the Convention on Biological Diversity and the United Nations Framework Convention on Climate Change, both of which focus almost exclusively on biodiversity and sustainability issues, and much less on culture or heritage. These models also frame products and outcomes within ecosystems-based and risk analyses models. Although the UNESCO TBR aims to protect Altai ecosystems and mitigate threats to biodiversity, the people who would be most affected, the local herders, were not a major part of negotiations. Instead, decisions were largely determined by Western experts, international heritage agencies, and the nation-state and were framed around archaeological and/or environmental values.

In my view, these studies foreground particular lines of investigation, namely, permafrost and archaeological data, cultural landscapes of ancient cultures, and the archaeology of Scythian cultures, while overlooking others. Such foci have profound consequences for local communities who remain largely outside of discussions related to heritage status. Does this create a bias whereby certain ideas are transposed onto these landscapes? How do these conceptions of value interfere with or contradict the value placed on these same landscapes by local communities who live and work in these high-mountain regions? I hold that in the making of heritage in the Mongolian Altai, specific views of the region—largely aesthetic, environmental, archaeological, and material—dominated the discussions and guided how the region would be managed and interpreted for a global audience.

The heritage landscapes of the Altai are presented in largely fragmented and partial ways. What have not yet been resolved are the impacts of UNESCO designations in these remote regions. Are the Altai heritage landscapes positioned to include intersecting, contradictory, or competing accounts of this place? If we are concerned about climatic changes and environmental stresses to the region, then have we thought through the consequences of increased tourism on nomadic herders' livelihoods? We do know that tourists have an impact on local herders today; how will increases in tourism coalesce with increasing climate variability, devastating droughts, extreme storms, and insecure water sources? These questions matter, and as we see in other regions of Mongolia, they are even more complicated now with the breathtaking increase of extractive industries that have reshaped Mongolia's free-market economy (Badenkov 2011; Plets et al. 2011). It is important to realize that these discussions revolve to some extent around heritage, and as we have seen in other contexts, World Heritage status has consequences for local stakeholders (see Baird 2009, 2013).

Environment/Culture/Heritage

A paper published in *Nature and Society* identified integrating studies on natural and cultural heritage as a key strategy in mediating environmental challenges (Pretty et al. 2009). Heritage landscapes are central to these discussions. As I argue here, it is important to tease these out beyond the scene of enactment, to show how landscapes are literally transformed through political posturing and rhetoric. However, our models and frameworks do not yet adequately provide a context to explore these tensions and intersections. Of course, one might object here that heritage scholars (or archaeologists or geographers, among others) are not tasked to take on these issues, or alternatively, that they do think about and work closely with communities. But I would counter that such remove is not intentional but is structured in the very way we present our work. Take for example the archaeological monograph, until recent years a requirement of any archaeological dissertation in North America. Most, including mine, begin with a detailed outline of the historical and social context of the site, then quickly shift gears to the matter at hand: assessment and analyses of the archaeological data. The sociopolitics of the site, if discussed, are largely relegated to footnotes or short discussions and are rarely given the prominent position they require. We also see this remove in heritage assessments and negotiations. When I prepared National Register nominations for two archaeological sites in Lake Clark National Monument, both of which were central to ongoing land claims, there was not a place to grapple with the politics of these sites in any meaningful way. It is true that the nomination requires consideration of significance, history of research, and so on, but at the same time, it does not provide a venue to discuss how these sites are also contested in the present, or more troubling, how the nomination could be used as evidence in the land claims negotiation. How can our projects also provide a place to take on the meatier and equally important issues?

To be clear, I am aware that heritage professionals and managers *do* grapple with and work to mediate these contexts. I make this point not simply to recognize this work but to underscore the constraints. My experiences working as an archaeologist for the Forest Service and National Park Service in Katmai and Lake Clark National Parks brought into sharp relief the challenges in addressing the multiple and competing claims and contexts of our work. Part of this is related to different missions, but it also concerns how we present our work in reports, National Register nominations, archaeological heritage surveys, environmental impact statements, and so on. In telling the stories of a particular place or archaeological culture, I have found that we often focus on the cultural or environmental contexts, previous histories of investigation, and/or the site's significance. There is less room for presenting the sociopolitical contexts and contemporary concerns.

In the examples presented in this chapter, I would argue that an opportunity to bring these concerns into our work was missed. In the Prince William Sound case, archaeologists were constrained by the larger project of conservation and cleanup. The priority was to protect the "most sensitive resources," even though there was not an agreement on what these resources were or how to protect them (Wells et al. 1995:5). What if archaeologists (and others) had been allowed to also bring in the contemporary concerns and conflicts and to make this part of the history and story of these places? A number of recent studies have done this to varied degrees (see, e.g., Gnecco and Ayala 2011; González-Ruibal 2008; R. Harrison 2011; Olsen and Pétursdóttir 2014). Such archaeology of the contemporary is shown in the Ruin Memories project, which places the archaeologist as practitioner at the center, with a concern for making sense of material remains, the assemblages left behind, and how these are contemporary sites of engagement. Archaeologists Bjørnar Olsen and Þóra Pétursdóttir (2014) draw on the metaphor of ruin to bring in ethics, capitalism, and the politics of heritage (see also Benjamin 2003). It is precisely this commitment to locating how archaeological ruins are enmeshed in the contemporary material world that offers a reassessment. I think the rapprochement I am searching for in the Alaskan and Mongolian contexts could be well served by thinking through these models from scholars of modern ruins and especially in repositioning the sociopolitical contexts and structures at work.

There is no doubt that such an approach would present an important perspective, one that takes seriously how local communities struggled with cleanup efforts as well as the subsequent health and economic burdens. But in my estimation, such an approach must also consider external and funding constraints. In the Prince William Sound example, we see how Exxon constrained the foci of studies and prevented discussions that overlap disciplinary boundaries by defining how funds were allocated and which studies were undertaken. In the heritage landscapes of the Sound, what constituted a "resource" was narrowly defined, resulting in the cultural resources receiving little or no attention from researchers and decision makers. Whether this was intentional cannot be known. In the Altai example, a valuable lesson could also be gleaned. The focus on material cultural, and specifically on threats to archaeological heritage, overshadowed the lived concerns of the indigenous Altains. The approach I propose here would bring in their voices and concerns, as they have long-term insights into the rapidly changing environments. Integrating their knowledge could provide unique data that could be used to mitigate the environmental changes and offer a much-needed perspective that is absent from many discussions.

A few challenges in this type of approach must be recognized. Clearly, determining what types of data to include is anything but simple; such a determination is, in fact, a selective process. As described in the next chapter, there is often little coherence in how agencies define heritage resources or identify problems. Engendering constructive engagement would require improving practices, strategies, outreach, and policies beyond a narrowly focused concern with habitats or restoration projects. In other contexts, scientists and land managers recognize uncertainty and risk, and actually build these into their environmental assessment models. Perhaps such an approach could be applied in cultural landscape contexts that could offer insights and strategies to address some of these "wicked" problems, a point I return to later.

4

Experts and Epistemologies

Of course those files are secret. We do that
so experts can write what they want.

Member of ICOMOS Secretariat, 2008 interview

Maybe it is just my ignorance but I fail to understand
why our land is being controlled in France anyway.

Letter from Tasmanian Aboriginal man
to the World Heritage Committee, 1988

ICOMOS Sixteenth General Assembly and
Scientific Symposium, Quebec, Canada, 2008

In 2008, I attended the General Assembly meeting of ICOMOS in Quebec. I
had traveled to the meeting as part of a larger research project that examined
the nature of expert knowledge, especially in the context of World Heritage
Indigenous cultural landscapes (see Baird 2009). I sought to "study up," and
my ethnographic, archival, and discourse analyses looked directly at decision
makers and those who wielded power in heritage negotiations (after Nader
1972). The project investigated how institutional and expert knowledge was applied in developing World Heritage nominations. I hypothesized that analyses
of the cultural landscape nomination process could provide a unique vantage
to investigate basic assumptions under which heritage experts operate. In recent years, landscapes have become the lingua franca of social scientists and
heritage managers. At the time of my study, the World Heritage Centre, the U.S.
National Park Service, and the European Union, for example, had all adopted
cultural landscapes as a category of heritage, and experts were critical to guiding
these organizations on best practices and on developing policy and management frameworks, guidelines, and standards to manage landscapes. Although
I was an international expert for ICOMOS and a registered participant for the
ICOMOS-IFLA (International Federation of Landscape Architects) Scientific

Meeting, I was asked to leave. Ten minutes into the meeting, the president announced that only voting members would be allowed to observe the morning session. When I asked about the sudden change, I was told that committee matters would "be of no interest to outside observers."

As I learned, studying up was not easy. The backstory to this abrupt meeting change was disclosed to me later in the day. Upon hearing that I was observing the meeting as part of my research on heritage experts, one member recommended that the meeting be closed. This would ensure that outside evaluators could not share or observe how decisions were made. I was not surprised, as I had encountered roadblocks at many points of my research. In my preliminary research trip to UNESCO and ICOMOS in Paris, for example, I found that in order to get access to nomination dossiers I had to first become an international expert recognized by these organizations (see Figure 4). When I returned the

Figure 4. Archives at UNESCO, Paris, photo by author.

following year newly credentialed as an expert member of the ICOMOS Scientific Committee and the International Committee on Archaeological Heritage Management, I was still largely prevented from accessing the archives in some subtle and not-so-subtle ways: missed meetings, lost files, conflicting e-mails and phone calls, and misinformation about which agency was responsible for finding the information and files I sought. It took an uncomfortable exchange in the archivist's office to finally gain access to the files I requested. Still, what at first felt personal, I later realized, was more likely related to what I termed then as institutional gatekeeping, an important theme that emerged in my work, and the subject of this chapter.

What experts say and do matters. Heritage experts comprise an interconnected group of professional practitioners, political actors, and bureaucrats who are central to the business of heritage. Their influence extends well beyond the conservation and management of natural or cultural heritage sites or cultural property: experts endorse and campaign, promote and shape opinions, and influence policy at all levels of government. The social scientist Michael Cernea, for example, has written, for the World Bank, key policy documents and scholarly work that outline the importance of cultural heritage for urban development (see, e.g., Cernea 2001). Although Cernea sees cultural heritage as a tool to reduce poverty, how this works in practice remains an open question. A number of authors have shown how such economic interventions also work in ways that harm communities and create inequalities (see, e.g., Comaroff and Comaroff 2009; Guarnaccia 2015; Welsh 1997). Webber Ndoro, director of the African World Heritage Fund, for example, called attention to well-meaning development schemata at heritage sites in Africa that are promoted as economic drivers but which mostly benefit foreign operators (Ndoro 2015). Although a number of studies have examined the tension between professional expertise and practice (see Baird 2009; Luke and Kersel 2013; Meskell 2015b; Titchen 2013; Turtinen 2000), we know very little about the wider relationships among heritage expertise, claims of ownership, authenticity, and identity. Although a full discussion of heritage expertise lies beyond the scope of this chapter, I aim to show that examining the culture of expertise is key to understanding how knowledge is produced and how expertise is applied in contexts beyond the more traditional remit of heritage.[1]

My review of the documents and ethnographic research revealed that how heritage experts constructed knowledge, how they related to, used, and reworked discourses, and how these were operationalized largely related to their disciplinary and professional backgrounds. The multiple theories and methods that are brought to bear in interpreting cultural landscapes, what I refer to as the "epistemologies of landscapes," intersect with issues related to cultural and natural heritage, landscape preservation, and identity.[2] The challenge for descendant and stakeholder communities is that these models often limit whose interests are defined and legitimized in how landscapes are imagined and defined (Baird 2009). Much of this relates to ideas of landscapes originating within a modern and Western framework. Such conceptions of landscapes cannot adequately accommodate Indigenous peoples' conceptions of landscapes, even in cases where these have been developed for community-based management (see Baird 2009). These limitations are especially pronounced in environmental heritage contexts where a narrow focus on conservation reifies the boundaries between nature and culture.

Environmental experts are increasingly active in heritage policy negotiations. They not only provide expertise and advice on how to manage protected areas, such as designated wilderness, wildlife refuges, or protected public lands, but also provide expertise to agencies that promote development and/or mitigate mining claims and activities (see Coombe and Baird 2015). Yet cultural heritage is often not identified in these models or is an adjunct to the real work at hand: global environmental governance. Such a strict focus on nature/environmental conservation can occlude how heritage landscapes are also political, social, and cultural. Although some may disagree with my assessment, I see this singular focus especially pronounced in ecosystems services and natural capital, both approaches that seek to sustainably manage and/or conserve nature. These frameworks have become a currency that multinational corporations, nation-states, private-sector NGOs, and others draw on in their decisions and management. As I aim to show, although these approaches identify stakeholders and may even implement community-based management plans, the focus on biodiversity conservation and natural resource management can also overlook how heritage is central to the work of conservation and larger environmental initiatives. Although cultural services are listed as an important "value," there are numerous barriers to their inclusion in decision making (see, e.g., Chan et al. 2011, 2012). Whatever the case, these frameworks require a broader conception and recognition of heritage.

The Culture of Expertise

Increasingly, anthropologists and other social scientists have turned their attention to experts (see Boyer 2005; Carr 2010; Holmes and Marcus 2007). Drawing from a range of approaches, from feminist theory and constructed identities, to Michel Foucault's conceptions of governmentality and biopower, to Bruno Latour's investigations of scientific facts (Latour and Woolgar 1979), these studies examine how expertise, in its broadest outlines, manifests in technology (Ong and Collier 2007), science (Hayden 2003; Helmreich 2009), medicine (Zhan 2009), energy (Mason and Stoilkova 2012; Tilt 2015), and security (Lakoff 2008). Yet, as anthropologist Dominic Boyer (2008:41) rightly warns, there is an inherent circularity (and irony) in anthropological studies of experts, because expertise is positioned in ways that can restrict access or "police ethnographic and theoretical content" (2008:43). Clearly, these tensions will not be easily resolved. But without lessening his critique, I suggest that in some contexts the benefits may outweigh the risks.

Recent work around extractive transnational corporations, for example, has provided unique insights and circumvented (at least some) these concerns by showing how expertise is enacted in practice (after Carr 2010). A new wave of scholars is working to map the complex and shifting terrain around extractive transnational corporations (see, e.g., Breglia 2013; Rajak 2011; Sawyer 2004; Welker 2014). Discarding abstractions (i.e., corporations, mining companies) for particulars and situated geographies, these studies contribute to our understanding of how expertise works in practice. This work, deeply ethnographic but also historical, investigates how expertise is mediated through transnational actors—corporations, NGOs, energy brokers—to provide a view beyond mere routines and regulations. Take, for example, anthropologist Marina Welker's (2014) engaging study of a global mining company in Indonesia. Her study challenged the notion of corporations as monoliths by demonstrating how the corporation embodied personhood. As her data suggest, the corporation was mutually constituted through struggles with local communities and engagements with workers, activists, local governments, and shareholders. Elsewhere, Arthur Mason and Maria Stoilkova (2012:85) engaged with expertise in a different way, through their conceptualization of what they term the "corporeality of expertise." They demonstrated how expertise is viewed as a commodity that Arctic resource sectors draw on in developing and promoting their interests. We see a similar strategy in South Africa. As anthropologist Dinah Rajak (2011:239) showed through her long-term ethnographic research, expertise was deployed in corporate social responsibility (CSR) initiatives that repositioned transnational mining corporations as "agents of progress and development." Collectively, these studies provide fine-grained ethnographic investigations and a glimpse "behind the curtain" that produce new understandings of corporate agents and experts. By decentering implicit narratives, they show how expertise is produced, challenged, and embodied in commonsense practices or is legitimized through structures of power.

What heritage experts do (and don't do), for whom, and why, is of note.

Think about the work they do: experts map, assess, manage, protect, value, identify, define, evaluate, appraise, and promote. Many of these activities are mediated and supported through laws, policies, and practices that aim to protect. Ironically, laws that govern these activities can also steer precariously close to strategies that police, restrict, and control. Consider the discourse of heritage. As Laurajane Smith (2006:11) has argued, heritage practitioners mobilized around specific definitions (and discourses) of heritage that promoted what she termed an "authorized heritage discourse" that relied on the "power/knowledge claims of technical and aesthetic experts, and is institutionalized in the state cultural agencies." This matters, because the institutionalization of heritage expertise occludes how discourses are historically situated and mediated within relations of power. Take, for example, the World Heritage list, an inventory of heritage sites deemed of "universal" significance. The list is generated largely by Western experts and inevitably prioritizes some sites to global significance while overlooking others. As Sophia Labadi (2007) demonstrated in her analysis of World Heritage nominations, experts more often promoted official or national discourses. The result? As I have argued elsewhere (Baird 2009), in the making of World Heritage, certain voices are excluded. In postcolonial contexts, such hegemonic discourses can take on a more troubling nature and become an extension of the colonial project (see, e.g., Long 2000).

It is also important to note that expertise is assumed in heritage practice. Think about archaeologists' ardent commitment to steward the past (see, e.g., Wylie 2002). Such a commitment does not originate from any moral obligation, but instead is built into the laws, practices, and policies of the discipline. As Laurajane Smith (2004) has argued, archaeologists have drawn on their role as stewards to gain credibility as professional experts (see also Carman 2000; L. Smith 2006). Although some scholars may be uneasy with this characterization, I believe that her assessment is an important intervention in the stewardship ethic. We know that the stewardship ethic is not always welcome; the idea that outsiders (e.g., archaeologists, heritage managers, geographers, museum specialists, park personnel) have authority and, more importantly, an obligation to steward and protect heritage has been challenged (see, e.g., Byrne 1991; Schmidt 2006; Silverman and Ruggles 2007). Tensions emerge, for example, when competing values come into conflict, as demonstrated when Australian Aborigines repainted their ancestral pictographs, a documented practice, and were accused of desecrating the "heritage of all mankind" (Bowdler 1988:520). Although most archaeologists were quick to stand in support of the rights of Indigenous people in this context, some did not (see, e.g., Rosenfeld 1989).

But we also see how the stewardship ethic can elide social and political realities and/or obstruct scholars from taking action to protect local communities. This is certainly true in the case of the salvage archaeological project related to the construction of the Merowe Dam on the Nile River in Northern Sudan. As archaeologists Claudia Näser and Cornelia Kleinitz (2012) described, archaeologists had been working in Dar al-Manisar to collect data before it was destroyed, but by the third year of the project all archaeological work was terminated. It is a complicated story, but as it is told, the local community invoked human-rights abuses and aimed much of the heat of their anger at archaeologists, who they claimed were insensitive to their concerns, especially concerns related to resettlement (see also Hafsaas-Tsakos 2011). Näser and Kleinitz (2012:287–288) view the larger issue not as the loss of archaeological data but instead as archaeologists' insistence that the "documentation of archaeological heritage . . . is a universal goal." In other words, generally well-meaning archaeologists failed to consider the larger sociopolitical stakes. Archaeologists had misconstrued warm interactions with local communities as synonymous with a serious engagement, and failed to recognize that the community was fully struggling to protect their rights. But, I see this failure to connect with the larger sociopolitical contexts of the project as systemic and embedded in how we do our work. And this example shows how stewardship is not a "universally accepted" activity. Invoking the right to protect cultural resources without careful consideration of how a community may be struggling with larger concerns can have unintended consequences. We do know that the number of development-induced displacement and resettlement projects and initiatives is increasing due to climate change, urban renewal, extractive industries, and tourism (see, e.g., Maharaj and Crosby 2013; Oliver-Smith 1996, 2009; Reedy-Maschner and Maschner 2013). A recognition of how our work and position as heritage experts intersects with infrastructural expansion or ecological and cultural concerns, or how it advances national government or private interests, must be integrated into our practice.

Heritage experts are perhaps more commonly associated with the global heritage arena, where an array of representatives of international governing bodies and brokers (e.g., UNESCO, IUCN, the World Bank) set the agenda and create the architecture of heritage governance. From technical experts in the field to management and policy makers, experts influence and shape specific views and values. Scholars have long debated the impact of experts in these contexts (see, e.g., Baird 2009; Cleere 2001; Fowler 2004; Labadi 2007; L. Smith 2006). Some have objected that international heritage bodies have been unfairly targeted and that in World Heritage contexts, for example, the true power to negotiate rests with the nation-state. As Lynn Meskell (2013) has cogently argued, the real decision makers are the signatories to the World Heritage Convention, not the governing bodies. To be sure, some critiques (including mine) of these heritage bodies have lapsed into somewhat reductive assessments and Meskell provides an important corrective to those who misplace the true power in these negotiations. Clearly, distinctions do matter. But at the same time, experts *do* analyze, broker, and mediate on behalf of international governing bodies and their expertise *does* impact and play a major role. As I have argued elsewhere, IUCN experts campaigned to restructure and reword the World Heritage natural criteria in the Operational Guidelines, which resulted in the denial of the 1986 cultural heritage nomination for Tongariro National Park in New Zealand (Baird 2009, 2015). The issue really comes down to power and control. Expert knowledge is a privileged position that is policed and protected.

Expertise is also shaped by assessments by archaeologists, museum workers, cultural heritage practitioners, and other nongovernmental actors. Such experts perform assessments, site visits, and nominations and rely on technical aspects and/or cultural significance to guide their work. Technical approaches can work to obscure the sociopolitical contexts.

Anthropologists Christina Luke and Morag Kersel (2013:13) have added another important context: heritage scholars who are "embedded agents in U.S. soft power and unofficial, long-term cultural diplomats" (see also Scham 2009). The positioning of cultural heritage ambassadors may appear, at first glance, as apolitical or perhaps serving nationalist or humanitarian aims. But such engagements take on a different tenor when one considers how expertise—of cultures, places and landscapes, and material culture—could also unknowingly serve as the handmaiden for a government's military, economic, or political objectives. Without a doubt, the positioning of heritage experts as cultural ambassadors can unwittingly place them in compromising positions. These contexts raise important questions about objectivity and ethics; heritage scholars would be well served in anticipating some of the uneven terrain of heritage expertise.

Heritage experts are increasingly working in development contexts. The World Bank, for example, employs a range of heritage experts in its urban-renewal projects. The Cultural Heritage and Urban Development Project in Lebanon draws on the country's cultural heritage to support economic development and enhance quality of life around historic centers."[3] Based on the World Bank's country assistance strategy for Lebanon, the project emphasizes the twin goals of preserving built heritage and developing tourism (see Al-Hagla 2010). The project mobilizes private investments and draws on technical expertise and is the centerpiece to poverty alleviation. The World Bank sees investing in tourism, which clearly draws on the cultural heritage value of the historic cities, as a way to promote economic and urban development. A range of experts, including landscape architects, archaeologists, and conservators, compete for contracts to rehabilitate the city centers. The city of Saida, for example, is developing a heritage trail that aims to celebrate the city's history and heritage. Nevertheless, this project will likely involve relocating people and businesses and will result in private investment, gentrification, and removal. In the process of "enhancing the quality of life," this urban-renewal project will inevitably change the cultural character and identity of the neighborhoods and the lives of the people who live there.

Heritage expertise is also enacted in ways that contribute to inequality and rights violations (Baird 2014; Byrne 1996). This is especially true in projects where the mandate is framed in terms of poverty reduction and/or environmental remediation. Much like the archaeologists working to protect archaeological resources in the Fourth Nile Cataract Region in Sudan, conservation experts working on urban-renewal or poverty eradication projects may not recognize that their work intersects with heritage assessments or may be prevented from addressing these in any meaningful way. Consider the Jordan Cultural Heritage, Tourism, and Development Project supported by the World Bank. At issue are the urban infrastructure and cultural landscape improvements that threaten neighborhoods. Local communities are outraged over potential resettlement and loss of homes and view the project as a "development disaster" (after Oliver-Smith 2009; see Guarnaccia 2015). Yet, in the promotion of tourism and urban development, market determinations take priority, and heritage is framed in tourism-friendly ways.[4] More troubling, however, is that experts in such circumstances may lack the language, historical context, or political mobility to address critiques or rights violations. In the next section I discuss a few of these contexts as they relate to ecological resources and capital-intensive development.

The "Wealth of Nature"

Heritage is central to most conservation and sustainable development initiatives, yet is often overlooked. Take, for example, the twentieth anniversary of the historic Earth Summit in Rio de Janeiro in 2012, where nations signed the legally binding Convention on Biological Diversity, the guiding framework for policy and research on biodiversity.[5] The Earth Summit was one of the first key environmental events to champion Indigenous cultural heritage and intellectual property rights. Twenty years later, world leaders, scientists, Indigenous peoples, environmentalists, and other interested people convened again in Rio de Janeiro at Rio+20, to address issues of sustainable development and environmental protections. Yet, unlike the first meeting, attention to culture and heritage were noticeably absent in discussions. In fact, members of the International Work Group on Indigenous Affairs (IWGIA) criticized the final Rio+20 report for not addressing culture.[6]

The underestimation of heritage is significant. Heritage engages a global network of experts who testify, provide opinions, and are sanctioned by the nation-state and other governing bodies to negotiate and make decisions involving heritage sites. Their expertise bears directly on research, planning, and policy discussions on heritage landscapes. Not only do experts provide technical advice, inform decision makers, and mediate boundary disputes; they also provide opinions and testify in land-rights claims, urban-renewal projects, World Heritage nominations, water rights claims, and ecosystem inventories. Without a doubt, many of these contexts are contested and not entirely free from political influence. So far, we know very little about how these professionals enact expertise in their work or research (but see Baird 2013; Coombe and Baird 2015; Meskell 2015a).

Heritage scholars should pay close attention to two intersecting environmental frameworks and initiatives that have broad traction and influence in heritage contexts: ecosystems services and natural capital. Ecosystems services, defined in the 2005 Millennium Ecosystem Assessment, are "the benefits that functioning ecosystems provide to people" and include such things as water, flood control, climate regulation, nutrient cycling, carbon sequestration, recreation, and tourism.[7] This guiding framework integrates experts from the natural and social sciences to identify, measure, map, or model these services and their trade-offs. Ecosystems services have been widely adopted, and their application can be found at all levels of government, academia, law, and industry.[8] Natural capital extends ecosystems services to consider the economic capital or the value of nature. Gretchen Daily, a key architect of this approach and senior fellow at the Woods Institute for the Environment at Stanford University, explained ecosystems services as the "benefits that flow from natural capital" (Daily 2013, personal communication). In other words, natural capital is an environmental accounting that "values" nature by making "conservation profitable" (after Daily and Ellison 2002). Of course, valuing environments and mediating impacts are critical to the health and well-being of our planet. At the same time, such services are difficult to price, and some have critiqued these models for their overconfident projections and/or their "blind faith in financial markets" (Conniff 2012; see also Ingram et al. 2012; Schröter et al. 2014).

To be clear, the contributions of ecosystems services and natural capital to environmental accounting cannot be dismissed; these initiatives share a deep concern for and commitment to addressing global environmental challenges. At the same time, Nature (not nature) trumps culture. While it is true that the Millennium Ecosystem Assessment defined cultural services as a key category of investigation, and the natural capital approach views stakeholders as essential to identifying and resolving conflict, these distinctions are not the same as a particular and complex understanding of culture(s). The calculus is quantitative and framed *around* ideas of nature and ecology: these models prioritize biodiversity and sustainability at the expense of culture. What should raise some alarms, as well, is how these models share similarities (and a genealogy) with earlier conservation strategies that displaced communities as a way to protect nature (Cernea and Schmidt-Soltau 2006; Igoe 2004).[9] The question remains: In what ways do experts draw on ideas of the "wealth of nature" to frame and order, select or obscure, promote or demote culture (Baird 2015)? How does one determine the "socio-cultural dimension of critical natural capital" (see, e.g., Chiesura and de Groot 2003)? Are there adequate checks and balances in these models to address competing claims and interests or think through where nature and culture collide?

A point not often acknowledged is that many of the "services" in ecosystems services or "capital" in natural capital are also heritage. Take for example the Payments for Ecosystems Services Program, which provides incentives to stakeholders who can provide an ecosystems service. In Tanzania, one wildlife safari tour operator outside of Tarangire National Park contracted the Maasai "to protect wildlife and to maintain grasslands for wildlife and livestock grazing" (Ingram et al. 2012:3–4). The Maasai are compensated for protecting a particular "cultural ecosystem service," that is, wildlife and grazing areas. But something is slightly amiss here. The cultural and natural heritage of the Maasai is framed as a service that is clearly of value to tour operators and tourists. But I wonder: Do the Maasai see it this way? We do know that they have had a long history of land alienation and insensitive treatment by anthropologists, missionaries, administrators, settlers, and traders (see Hughes 2006). It would be important to make clear how heritage maps onto these services and if this program extends on earlier intrusions and stereotypes of Maasai culture.

Once we start to see heritage in this way—that is, embedded within larger developments or environmental initiatives—we will see how these contexts are intensifying. IUCN, perhaps better known for its heritage advisory role to UNESCO's natural heritage and cultural landscape nominations to the World Heritage list, also partners with industry, governments, and NGOs on a variety of programs of consequence to heritage. IUCN's Global Protected Areas Programme is an obvious example. This program conserves "nature with associated ecosystem services and cultural values," and their inventory of protected areas includes numerous sites of cultural significance to Indigenous communities.[10] Ontario's Pukaskawa National Park, for example, is a protected area along the shores of Lake Superior and is the former territory of the Anishinaabeg First Nations. The history of the park is not without controversy, and relationships between the park and Aboriginal groups have been historically and politically tense. Although many of these issues have been resolved, with the adoption of the protected areas program, management of the park must now adhere to objectives that align with those set out in the Convention on Biological Diversity and the Millennium Development Goals. This, in itself, is not an issue, but it does place interpretation and management of cultural heritage within an environmental frame.

But, equally compelling and clearly intersecting are IUCN's engagement on natural capital initiatives in Aboriginal contexts. The IUCN–Rio Tinto Natural Capital Project in Western Australia seeks to "assess and value the ecosystem impacts of dewatering in the mining industry."[11] As discussed in previous chapters, the heritage of water and importance to Aboriginal communities and care of Country cannot be overstated (see, e.g., Somerville 2013). At issue are how the mining activities occur on important lands of the Traditional Owners, yet the project report does not identify the work that is being done as intersecting with or affecting the cultural or natural heritage. The relationship to local communities is conceptually abstracted, and its historical contexts are ignored. The controversies over the establishment of the Marandoo mine in Karijini National Park, amid protests by Traditional Owners, for example, were about care of Country. In that case, Hamersley Iron pushed for an exemption in the Aboriginal Heritage Act 1972 and was the impetus for mining companies, and in particular, Rio Tinto, to adopt proactive approaches to work with and represent the interests of Indigenous Australians (Scambary 2013). That the IUCN–Rio Tinto Natural Capital Project did not address Country in discussions of the impacts of dewatering is an oversight. In stronger terms, framing water as a resource or service removes its context as heritage and integral to Aboriginal Country. This idea, reframing Country as a resource, will be developed in the next chapter.

Epistemologies of Landscapes

In 2011, I traveled through Kakadu National Park in the Northern Territory of Australia. I had only a short time, so I hired an Aboriginal guide to visit Jim Jim

Billabong in an area called Yellow Water. When we arrived at the site, we spent about thirty minutes standing around (I was scanning for crocodiles) until he said, "This is my mother's story." I cannot recall the details of the story, but I do remember how the story and the place connected him to his ancestors, to plants and animals and seasons, to fire and ceremony, and the Dreaming. I have heard similar sentiments shared before, by a member of the Council of Katmai Descendants whose ancestral lands are today part of Katmai National Park, or by the tribal preservation officer for the Cheyenne River Sioux, during our traditional cultural property assessment for Agate Fossil Beds National Monument. In each case, place and landscape figure prominently in how people define themselves and their relationship to the world. My thinking about landscapes has been shaped by these stories, as well as by books and classes, research and exploration, and trial and error. In a beautifully felt book on Aboriginal Australia, Margaret Somerville (2013) shows how ideas of place are tied to Country. In the drought-prone landscape of the Murray-Darling Basin, one of the driest places on Earth, Somerville uses deep mapping and ethnography to show the centrality of water in Country and beyond. She also illustrates how such understandings are not easily come by, but require patience, time, and the ability to reach across language and cultural barriers. In her research, such patience and commitment revealed how place was not a location on a map but instead tied to story lines and Country, art and landscape, water and language. Her research in the Murray-Darling Basin has far-reaching lessons concerning the centrality of Indigenous understandings of landscapes and place and especially how these can contribute to contemporary debates over culture and environment.

What are the politics of making place? Although Western scholars have captured these senses of place, or how place is imbued with wisdom and meaning, our understandings provide only a fragmented and partial view (after Basso 1996). I may not understand the genealogical connections to place, but I do recognize that such knowledge is fiercely protected. One way to protect these stories is to recognize how heritage expertise, and its heavy reliance on Western concepts of time and place, can interfere with Indigenous understandings of place. This is not a critique of the work but rather an observation of how deeply embedded ideas of materiality and aesthetics infuse our understandings. The multiple theories and methods that experts bring to bear in interpreting cultural landscapes have consequence. The position, theoretical training, and goals of a researcher direct the focus and outcome of a study. When considering the consequences of applying these models to non-Western or Indigenous contexts, we must keep in mind that the majority of models we use and borrow from were developed within a modern and Western framework. Even in cases where scholars have had extraordinary access to communities, there is always a cultural distance. What are the implications for managing heritage places?

To think about this question, I will frame this discussion around the World Heritage cultural landscape category created in 1992, developed in part to address disparities and the over-representation of Western European sites and natural heritage properties and the under-representation of Indigenous peoples' heritage. A good illustration of the challenges related to expertise and World Heritage cultural landscape is the 1995 nomination of the Republic of the Philippines terraces to the World Heritage Committee as a World Heritage cultural landscape, a site promoted for its traditional rice terrace farming, sustainable practices, and a "landscape of great beauty that expresses the harmony between humankind and the environment."[12] Ifugao scholars Rachel Guimbatan and Teddy Baguilat (2006:61) noted that the nomination was resisted and resented. Why? In part, because their traditional practices were reframed to fit World Heritage values, but also because the rice terraces were not sustainable, and experts did not adequately address the sociopolitical contexts: the colonial histories, the impacts of Christianity, and the legacies of violent policies under sustained Spanish and American rule that transferred decision making to government agencies and away from traditional leadership (Gonzalez 2000:100). Even after independence in 1946, the Ifugao were marginalized in the country's rebuilding efforts. With inscription of the "living" cultural landscapes of the Philippines Cordilleras to the World Heritage list, the Ifugao were literally frozen in time and relegated to perform for a global audience. Unable to sustain their traditional farming practices, they out-migrated, and in 2001 the heritage landscape was placed on the List of World Heritage in Danger, with nearly 30 percent of the terraces abandoned and subsequently damaged. Although the site has since been removed from this list, communities struggle with mass tourism, urban sprawl, watershed destruction, and deforestation, while at the same time reconciling global attention with local needs (UNESCO 2008:vii).

Experts' positions, theoretical training, and goals weigh heavily on the focus and outcome of a study. In the Philippines example, experts shaped their ideas of landscapes around aesthetics, sustainability, and universal value, and in isolation of the larger historical and political contexts. The way the nomination was presented, experts could not fully account for the Ifugaos' participation in the global economy and the effects of colonial policies. Sovereignty did not alleviate the legacy of violent colonial rule, and in any case, the Ifugao were cut off from

their families and prevented from maintaining their lands and traditional practices. Still, some heritage managers today support developing tourism industries
as a way to "revive disappearing cultural practices" (UNESCO 2008:vii). Without addressing the fallout from colonialism, it is more likely, however, that the
increased attention to heritage will continue to disrupt the community's ecological, economic, and cultural connection to the terraces.

These tensions call attention to the need to examine how experts deploy ideas
of landscapes (or nature, wilderness, or sustainability for that matter) in their
conceptualizations of heritage. As I have argued elsewhere, ideas of heritage are
largely determined through the agendas and recommendations of the nation-
state, Western experts, and international heritage agencies and are framed to
fit specific World Heritage values (Baird 2009). This happens on a few fronts.
First, ideas of what constitutes the heritage inventory trace back to notions of
what is valued. This could be environments or aesthetics or wilderness as a ref-
uge or sanctuary. Yet, as anthropologist Julie Cruikshank (2005) showed in her
ethnographic study of the Saint Elias Mountains (now part of a transboundary
UNESCO World Heritage site between Canada and the United States), such
competing ideas often collide. In that case, early explorers, scientists, and environmental activists (including John Muir) transposed their ideas of Nature
(sublime, inanimate, a resource) onto the landscape. These early and contested
visions of Nature are today built into legal agreements, policies, and practices
that govern and direct how the park is managed. Without a doubt, the stakes for
descendant communities are high.

Ideas of landscapes tend to redefine Indigenous knowledge practices and
cultural traditions as heritage resources and/or promote these for their aesthetic, scenic, or natural values (see Baird 2009). The World Heritage cultural
landscape category, for example, lists many sites linked to European national
identity, such as vineyards and historic gardens, with only a handful representing Indigenous landscapes. This could relate, in part, to the constitution of the
scientific committee in charge of cultural landscapes. The UNESCO scientific
committee on cultural landscapes, the IFLA, advises the World Heritage Committee and conveys specific visions of cultural landscapes that likely originate
from their professional interests and activities as architects, landscape architects,
and art historians (Baird 2009). When used to interpret Indigenous landscapes,
these visions may not fully recognize or address Indigenous understandings
of place, and they may have unfortunate consequences. Ideas of cultural landscapes, originating with ICOMOS-IFLA and IUCN and adopted by the World
Heritage Committee, are used to develop World Heritage nominations, and in

Indigenous cultural landscape contexts these ideas tend to reframe the Traditional Owners' understandings of place to fit World Heritage values.

It must also be recognized that the cultural landscape designation is a tool used for economic development by modern nation-states, state and local governments, parks, and tourism industries. The heritage values are showcased and marketed to national and international audiences. In some contexts, the potential impacts of this increased attention have not been addressed: commercialization or appropriation of Indigenous knowledge, desecration or violation of sacred or fragile sites, environmental impacts, displacement from lands, or the further erosion of Traditional Owners' ability to control their heritage. In my analyses of Tongariro National Park, for example, I found that placing economic values on the cultural landscape inventory reduced the Traditional Owners' rights to speak for or protect their culture and also violated their custodial responsibilities (Baird 2013). The Traditional Owners, the Ngāti Tūwharetoa, are concerned that the park did not protect their sacred sites. And, as I discussed in the context of Uluṟu–Kata Tjuṯa, the Traditional Owners have repeatedly fought to prevent visitors from climbing Uluṟu or accessing sacred sites. Without a doubt, promoting parks as heritage landscapes while at the same time implementing protections is challenging. Heritage experts in these contexts, knowingly or not, construct value and promote narratives that work to protect their authority. In Tongariro, the Traditional Owners were positioned outside of heritage management decision-making power, and because they could offer only expressive cultural identity, they could not regulate how their lands were managed. It is important to think about how information originates outside of local communities' systems of authority and knowledge; knowingly or not, scientists and World Heritage experts are positioned as decision makers and knowledge producers. Ideas of heritage originating from professional archaeologists can became enmeshed in institutional and political practices that legitimate and/or justify the subordinate status of Traditional Owners or, within a larger hierarchy of meaning, are determined by the nation-state. Even in cases where Traditional Owners are co-managers or advisers, they are not always positioned as experts in heritage negotiations.

The adoption of the cultural landscape designation and concept is one way that land managers and heritage experts seek to recognize culture and address the emphasis on nature. The cultural landscape inventory could include songs, oral traditions, memories, Dreaming tracks, languages, knowledge systems, archaeological sites, historic buildings, rock art, ecosystems, flora and fauna, geological formations, wetlands, and karsts, among others. Yet, what has not been fully addressed is how this expanded inventory positions experts along the full heritage continuum, in some cases outside of their expertise, training, or qualifications. In other professional contexts, such as medicine and engineering, specialists who provide expert witness testimonies are disciplined if they provide opinions outside of their expertise. Admittedly, this analogy is a stretch, but not if one considers the political contexts. Experts might not have the skills, training, or cultural competence to work with some types of heritage included within the cultural landscapes inventory. During my study of the inventories of both Tongariro and Uluṟu–Kata Tjuṯa National Parks, I found that they included sacred sites, oral traditions, songs, and other sensitive material that, in many cases, should not be identified or discussed by outsiders. Yet in both cases, sensitive material was unintentionally made available to external audiences. Certainly, this breach of confidentiality is not specific to cultural landscapes, but the expanded inventory increases the chance that heritage managers could opine beyond their levels of expertise or reveal sensitive material that could violate Indigenous law or protocols.

As I asked previously, what are the cultural politics of nature and making place? Ideas of what constitutes place are often taken up in ways that efface complicated histories, presenting as natural what is in fact constructed. More importantly, *how* these ideas are used in heritage legislation or protection has consequences, as shown in the examples where outsiders (e.g., archaeologists, heritage managers, NGOs, and environmentalists) call upon their authority or obligation to steward and protect. There are clearly competing claims and tensions, and our understandings include values and assumptions that are neither neutral nor objective. Tropes of nature and conservation abound in heritage landscape contexts and influence laws, policies, and practices. Ideas of what constitutes the heritage inventory are constantly negotiated and reimagined. Therefore, it is critical that heritage scholars trace the epistemologies of landscapes—how they know what they know—within their work and understandings and that they think about how this knowledge shapes policies and practices. In recognizing that heritage is being called upon to do the work of environmental protections, it behooves us to understand how it is also historically and socially constructed. It is not enough to critique the flow of knowledge; it is necessary to grasp how it gains immediacy and relevancy, how it is used in crafting legislation, and ultimately, how it gains traction on the ground.

Gatekeeping

In this brief discussion I will draw from ethnographic and archival analyses related to the UNESCO-designated cultural landscape Tongariro National Park, in New Zealand. It is important to clarify that I am *not* attacking heritage experts. Instead, my aim is to call attention to how expert knowledge can mask power relations and/or minimizes conflict. One might object that my assessment misrepresents the true motivation of heritage experts. It is true that heritage experts *are* sensitive to how their knowledge is used and mobilized. What I am speaking specifically to is how this knowledge becomes institutionalized and protected, outside of critique or review. Or, alternatively, how certain ideas are promoted and policed to protect institutional or disciplinary perspectives.

Take, for example, the fact that the selection of experts in cultural landscape site missions and evaluations is not always transparent, though it is not clear why the names of the people making these decisions are not disclosed (Baird 2009). In the case studies I reviewed, I found that heritage managers at the local, state, national, and international levels were positioned as decision makers and knowledge producers, and Indigenous peoples' interests were for the most part secondary to these discussions, especially when these discussions deviated from institutional interests. I found that in Tongariro, although Maori interests were included in the park's management philosophies, they were not a priority. As such, Maori people's complex and multifaceted relationships to land were reframed as a relationship to the "natural" world (Baird 2013). Much of this relates to a misreading of *taonga,* defined here as "treasured possession." *Taonga* contains a tribe's historical memories and connects people to their land (see Henare 2007; Tapsell 1997). As I have argued elsewhere, lack of Indigenous representation or third-party review forces Indigenous groups to depend on heritage managers and *their* definitions and understandings of cultural landscapes, resulting in Indigenous peoples' knowledge and intellectual philosophies being misunderstood or, in more egregious cases, ignored.

A closed feedback loop exists in some heritage contexts, such that definitions of heritage are used by most members and placed beyond critique or review. The challenge for local communities is that this system is not set up to allow for stakeholders to evaluate the conduct or content of the research, the merit of the recommendations, the researchers' expertise or standpoints, or the impacts or consequences of the designation. Part of these issues relate to the bureaucracies that rely on an overwhelming array of policies, procedures, and guidelines. My study of internal negotiations not evident in final nominations showed how Tongariro's conservation director wrote to the IUCN president to discuss the removal of the cultural heritage criteria. A series of letters shows how IUCN representatives and park managers discussed reducing the burden of IUCN in matters related to cultural heritage. The IUCN's position was that natural heritage and cultural heritage values were largely incompatible and that coordinated activities were not necessary. Although ICOMOS and IUCN representatives share common interests, including promoting and improving heritage resources, reducing impacts on resources, and serving the needs of the World Heritage Committee, IUCN representatives felt that the advisory bodies duplicated efforts and did not exchange information. These discussions led to the restructuring and rewording of the World Heritage natural criteria in the Operational Guidelines and resulted in the denial of the cultural heritage values in the 1986 nomination. IUCN stressed the need for cooperation with ICOMOS and the desire to avoid duplicate efforts while pursuing common objectives. I suspect that IUCN representatives downplayed the relevance of cultural heritage because their mission is to promote natural heritage values. The dynamic tension between the advisory bodies could be related to the very different and somewhat incompatible visions of what constitutes the cultural landscapes inventory, and this may have consequences for Indigenous groups. Rather than harmonious relations and the pursuit of common goals, the internal debates strained already tenuous relations.

In many heritage contexts, a gatekeeping culture exists. By *gatekeeping* I refer to the policies, practices, and strategies that work to exclude third party or peer review, prevent alternative interpretations, and suppress opposition. Ideas and practices are subsumed within complex frameworks that tend to thwart dissent. Collective decision making primarily rests in the hands of a few, which masks struggles for power among stakeholders. Further, unlike other research contexts, some experts, such as those in World Heritage contexts, are not required to follow regulations for the protection of human subjects. Whether intentional or not, by excluding outside review, heritage practitioners defend and secure their positions as knowledge producers and decision makers. For example, a review of letters related to the nomination of Tongariro National Park show what the park documents did not: the Maori were marginalized from the nomination process and were frustrated by their lack of representation. A few letter writers argued that the committee had not shown sensitivity to their laws, customs, and beliefs. They argued that UNESCO representatives had not consulted them about access to their sacred sites, and they were concerned about the increased access and international attention that a World Heritage listing would bring. In 1987 a direct descendant of Chief Horonuku addressed the World Heritage Committee and stated that IUCN did not consult with Maori, who "would certainly not sanction this nomination." These data direct our attention to how certain voices were excluded. Overall, letters of protest appear to have had no impact on reports, summaries, and advisory body evaluations, nor were they considered in the nomination process. Further, until archaeologists sympathetic to the Maori peoples' position reported on the cultural heritage, advisory bodies largely defined the heritage value or significance of the park without fully consulting local and Indigenous stakeholders. The consequences were significant: Maori were not given a way to control or protect their sacred sites, nor were they able to interpret those sites for the public who would enter the park.

Clearly, expert knowledge is a privileged position and is vetted and protected. The story of the "Copper Country" in the Keweenaw Peninsula provides an illustration. Located in the Lake Superior Basin of Michigan, the region underwent enormous transformations with the copper and iron rushes in the 1800s and the bust in the 1970s. This region was central to "America's first mineral land rush" of companies and workers excavating the vast copper deposits, and it provided the architecture for other mining rushes throughout the United States (Hoagland 2010:1). In the southern region of the Upper Peninsula, vast iron ore deposits spawned industry, towns, ports, and wealth. The heritage of mining in the Upper Peninsula maps onto ideas of "iron men" and company towns, independence and economic growth.

I live today in the former mining town of Houghton, Michigan, and I see firsthand the impact of industry and what happens when the mines left: economic collapse, environmental degradation, and social decay. The post-industrial landscape includes milling sites and smelters, as well as extensive mine tailings and waste rock piles, whose significance as either toxic waste or cultural resource is ardently debated (see Quivik 2007). My property includes an abandoned mining trench and a towering metal sculpture perched atop the ancient basalt ridge, which I am told once held a gaslight to assist aerial mapmakers in surveying the region. The beauty of the Lake Superior watershed is marred by the impacts of global production and boom-and-bust cycles on local communities. The once-thriving company town, with its paternal promises of wealth, jobs, and industry, left only long-term economic struggles, urban decay, and a landscape dotted with toxic and Superfund sites. The people I have interviewed in my town and throughout the region struggle with reconciling these realities with the nostalgic and hard-held view that "mining is our history."

Despite these challenges, the industrial heritage landscapes of the region today celebrate "the story of Copper." This story was created through the efforts and expertise of archaeologists and historians who promoted the region's importance. Scrap metal drives in World War II took away some of the industrial remains; heritage manager Scott See (2013:6), an industrial historian, has referred to these remains as "symbols for the mining companies and a source of identity for the miners themselves." Today, extractive industries tap into this strong heritage identity to validate company interests and investment. These efforts, in part, re-sulted in the creation of the Keweenaw National Historical Park, whose office coordinates with numerous organizations in the interpretation of sites through-out the 800,000 acres of the peninsula. Specifically, after the mines closed in the 1970s, the National Park Service, among other heritage groups, became a major industry in the Upper Peninsula. In the 1990s, the Keweenaw National Histori-cal Park was established to celebrate the region's mining heritage. In the wake of mining, heritage organizations at the national, state, and local levels came in and developed a huge heritage network that taps into this mining history. As a heritage industry, the region boasts copper mine museums, mining heritage museums, a historic fort (which protected the region's copper resources during the Civil War), and mine tours.

Yet not all members of the community see the region as an industrial heri-tage landscape. In the way the region is interpreted, the role of Native people is largely ignored, despite the fact that the region is the ceded territory of the Anishinaabe. Moreover, the region is reeling with the toxic legacies of mining impacts, and heritage scholars and environmentalists ardently disagree about the management of some heritage, particularly tailing piles. Still others question why the focus is not on the wildness of Lake Superior. The heritage industry in the Copper Country was seen as a way to rebuild and bring money to the region. Many people's livelihoods and careers are tied to telling (and preserving) "the story of copper." But this story has a shadow side. The region is resurging with new and proposed mines aimed at extracting its mineral resources and wealth. What is new is how mining companies are mapping onto the well-hewn narra-tive that "mining is our heritage." In this context, we see how our ideas of heri-tage landscapes are taken up and used for other means. I suspect that the region is heavily invested in a particular story and that heritage experts protect their interests to tell this story. Without a doubt, the interpretation and management of heritage landscapes engage a suite of stakeholders, from individuals working for local or national heritage organizations to governments, industries, non-governmental or grassroots organizations, and international heritage bodies. It is crucial that our models locate heritage within this field of power and, more specifically, how it articulates with environmental decisions and strategies. As I will describe next, it is important to trace how ideas of heritage gain traction and are used by industry to sanction activities and gain legitimacy.

5

Landscapes of Extraction

They didn't ask the Aboriginal people here if that place had
a name already—and it had. Its name for thousands of years has
been Jarndunmunha: there's nothing nameless about that.

Tom Price, Yinhawangka elder, Western Australia

Darwin, Northern Territory, Australia, November 2011

We arrived in Darwin weary and worn. As I stepped outside into the hot, humid
night I was overcome with a feeling akin to what naturalist J. B. MacKinnon
(2015:2) once described as a "wave of raw fear, the sort you would feel if a cold
hand grabbed at your ankles as you swam in deep water." Clearly my senses were
heightened from jetlag and anticipation, but at that moment I was gripped with
doubt about the journey ahead: caravan from Darwin to the town of Onslow
in Western Australia's Pilbara region nearly three thousand kilometers away to
investigate how heritage landscapes are increasingly also sites of industry.[1] It
was not so much the distance that worried me but that we would be traveling
toward the remotest and hottest part of Australia with the summer and cyclone
seasons approaching. As we made our way into the stark and deeply connected
landscape, the foreboding receded and was replaced with something closer to
reverence. Through experiencing the hard fought-distances, the remoteness and
extremes, the light and shadows, we could sense more acutely the transformations occurring in the Pilbara. By the time we arrived outside of Port Hedland,
a deepwater mining port and hub, it was evident that something extraordinary
was taking place.

For more than fifty years, Western Australia has been a site of industry and
mining. But, in recent years, major resource projects, from iron ore and uranium to liquefied natural gas (LNG), have accelerated.[2] The unprecedented
scale of construction and development, coupled with escalating losses to environmental and cultural heritage, are phenomena that have consequences and

Figure 5. "Mount Nameless," or Jarndunmunha, Tom Price, Western Australia, photo by author.

costs. The Pilbara represents what Anna Tsing (2005; see also 2003) and others have termed a resource frontier, a conceptual category that at once references both the activities (i.e., investment, extraction, development) and the peoples and places in its reach. Industry is increasingly influencing heritage along the resource frontier. In Australia these contexts are announced by plans to dredge for coal near the Great Barrier Reef or expand uranium mining near World Heritage sites and sacred landscapes. Of note is how these same industrial heritage landscapes are Country to Aboriginal people.[3]

Frontiers are more than a metaphor, as they provide a framework to explore the transformations of Country or traditional territories by industry. Scholars have established how resources and lands are at the center of negotiations with stakeholder communities (Altman 2003; Altman and Martin 2009; Breglia 2013; Golub 2014; Golub and Rhee 2013; Haslam Mckenzie 2013; Kirsch 2006; Sawyer 2004; Scambary 2013)."[4] In the last decade there has been a marked increase of mining (and other) operations (iron ore, salt, aluminum, uranium, coal-bed methane and gas) on Indigenous lands or traditional territories.[5] In British Columbia in 2010, for example, the Haisla Nation of British Columbia entered into a thirty-year agreement with Rio Tinto Alcan to support aluminum operations and signed an agreement with the government to fast-track an LNG plant."[6] More recently, the Trudeau government is pushing to build the massive Pacific NorthWest LNG project that, once approved and built, will cut through the culturally rich and environmentally sensitive Great Bear Rainforest to reach a soon-to-be-built gas terminal on Lelu Island. The island is known as Lax U'u'la and is the traditional territory of Smʼogyet Yahaan and Lax Kw'alaams, who have set up a protest camp and are actively opposing the project in order to protect their lands and critical wild salmon populations. Unsurprisingly, these sites also map onto communities that have been historically disenfranchised or under-represented, and engagements are built on the well-grooved architecture of settler colonial policies that have yet to find resolution.

In these cases we see how heritage is newly configured along the resource frontier. Richard Howitt, an Australian researcher who was one of the earliest critics of industrialization as it relates to Indigenous rights, has shown how the approach of resource managers has rendered Indigenous peoples' values and knowledge systems as largely invisible, or at least outside of dominant approaches. Howitt (1992) showed how, in the development of an aluminum mine in Cape York, establishing strong relationships with Aboriginal people as community leaders worked to smooth negotiations. This is not always the case. In the Southeast Asian context, Tsing (2005:28) demonstrated how such an approach aligns with and supports a new spirit of corporate engagement that literally "disengaged nature from local ecologies and livelihoods." This means that the resource frontier provides the context for industries (and others) to negotiate access to raw materials and resources as well as changes in policy. As I explore in this chapter, part of this work is done through discourse. This is accomplished most specifically through creation of corporate discourse, a discourse that mediates ideas surrounding land and access, sustainable development, and the rights of Indigenous peoples to control and care for Country. Global mining giant Rio Tinto has been at the forefront of heritage discourse and developed the guide *Why Cultural Heritage Matters*, which presents their vision for engagements with Indigenous communities (Bradshaw and Rio Tinto 2011).[7] The guide serves as a go-to reference for all of its employees and affiliates. Although the language of community engagement, good governance, and partnerships infuses the guide, as I argue in this chapter, industry actors also draw on discourse in ways that serve their interests. As I have argued elsewhere, this discourse provides a context for industry (and others) to bridge discussions away from social and environmental concerns (Coombe and Baird 2015; see also

Luning 2012; Welker 2009, 2014).[8] Although scholars are working to capture these new engagements, the scope and pace are complicated and far-reaching and are often difficult to trace.

"We fight because we must": Industry and Heritage in the Burrup Peninsula

To get a better sense of the practices of extractive industries on the ground and the impacts of these activities on Indigenous communities and heritage, I traveled to sites in the Northern Territory and Western Australia. What caught my attention was the intensity of the resource boom in the Pilbara region of Western Australia.[9] The rush attracted a global workforce that provided the technologies, bureaucracies, and expertise to build the infrastructure, including deepwater ports, railways, and roads. Ironically, the Western Australian government had been supportive in developing the region's industry while at the same time promoting the area's heritage. Much like the histories of land alienation and restrictive assimilation policies for Traditional Owners of Uluṟu–Kata Tjuṯa National Park (described in chapter 1), the Traditional Owners of the Burrup have had to repeatedly fight to retain their lands and/or protect their traditional knowledges and practices. These experiences were often tense and violent and included indentured labor and missions, violence, and land alienation. Without diminishing the importance of these contexts, I concentrate here on recent engagements around resource industries and Indigenous communities as a way to think through how heritage is engaged in these negotiations. And much like the Uluṟu–Kata Tjuṯa example, the struggle in the Pilbara region is rooted in the control of Country.[10]

The Pilbara has a history of industry, pastoralism, mining, and pearling (see Scambary 2013). Industry has taken up this history to advance their interests. Glenn Albrecht and Neville Ellis (2014:43) have argued that the region's resource industry has promoted itself largely through the narrative of progress.[11] In fact, the Western Australian model of development was unique in that it was capital-intensive, requiring infrastructural development and large investment and support from the state government (Phillimore 2014:26). This model provided the architecture that is still in play in negotiations today, especially in the production and construction of the North West Shelf gas hub, which began in Karratha in the 1970s and resulted in the destruction of much of the most important petroglyph and sacred sites in Australia and Country to the Traditional Owners, the Ngarluma/Yindjibarndi, Yaburara Madudhunera, and Wong-Goo-tt-oo people.[12] The Burrup Peninsula, or Murujuga, includes Aboriginal sacred sites and environmentally sensitive coastal resources as well as an estimated nearly one million petroglyphs (Mulvaney 2013). The peninsula, until recently, was on the Australian National Heritage list, in consideration for potential nomination to the World Heritage list, and in 2014 the minister for environment announced the creation of Murujuga, Western Australia's one hundredth national park. The park was created, in part, to address critiques from Traditional Owners, as well as to mitigate the cultural and environmental heritage impacts of industry on the peninsula. Despite its strong connection to Traditional Owners, the majority of the peninsula is now an industrial estate.

The site of the industrial estate was the result of protracted negotiations. Ultimately, the land at issue was designated as non-industrial under a 2003 management plan between industry, government, and native title holders called the Burrup and Maitland Industrial Estates Agreement (see discussion in Edmunds 2013). Although some see the agreement as the "most comprehensive . . . ever made by any government with an Aboriginal group over land in Australia" (Flanagan nd; see also Edmunds 2013), it sets precedents in ways that have irrevocable and far-reaching repercussions for Traditional Owners. The agreement was rushed and by all accounts inevitable. As a lead negotiator for the negotiations, Frances Flanagan (nd:10) noted, "it was evident that neither the State nor the Ngarluma Yindjibardni people were likely to achieve their objectives by relying solely on the processes of the Native Title Act. The community knew that they were not able to stop the development by withholding their consent to it." Although the Traditional Owners were given many more negotiation rights—due to the WA Aboriginal Heritage Act and the Native Title Act—the pace and scope of the negotiations were accelerated to fast-track the multibillion-dollar energy project. Meanwhile, an independent review of the ethical context of the agreement found that it had failed to protect culture and biodiversity (Brueckner et al. 2014:8). Clearly, much was at stake, and much had already been promised and/or committed. Whatever the case, the implications of siting an industrial estate on a well-known and highly important sacred site that is also the site of the 1868 Flying Foam Massacre calls into question the power dynamics in negotiations.

The siting of an industrial estate on the Burrup Peninsula was the subject of heated debates between industry, local groups, rock art scholars, environmental NGOs, and Aboriginal groups. Many groups protested because the area is culturally important to the Traditional Owners (Bednarik 2011; Edmunds 2013; McDonald and Veth 2009). Nevertheless, the largest tenant, Woodside LNG, built Western Australia's first LNG plant on culturally and environmentally sensitive areas. They have also built the infrastructure to support access to the significant gas deposits and to bring these to the Dampier Port on the Burrup Peninsula, the name for the part of the Dampier Archipelago once known as Dampier Island (R. Davidson 2011). Murujuga National Park was created as part of the agreement and to address some of these issues, and is today jointly managed by the Department of Environment and Conservation (DEC) and the Murujuga Aboriginal Corporation under a management plan developed in consultation with the community and prepared by a council composed of Traditional Owners, DEC representatives, and the Minister of Indigenous Affairs.

But, while many may protest the cultural and environmental costs, there has also been a cost to heritage and Country. Despite their negotiations and recognition of the agreement, the people I talked with spoke to me in terms of loss and dispossession, not of gains and economic paybacks. I also observed how Country was taken up in discussions with mining representatives in ways that sought to showcase the latter's knowledge and respect for heritage and Country. Without a doubt, the people I spoke with had a deep sense of the importance of the Burrup Peninsula *as* Country, but something interesting occurred in how mining representatives talked about it. What I observed was how heritage was co-opted, in a way, to now serve industry interests. Yet, in my observations, the contested histories had been occluded (or assumed resolved), and conversations begin with the new technologies and new landscapes of the Pilbara. As I suggest, Country has been transformed into a resource and now serves as a prop to showcase energy infrastructures and technologies.

Industry Engagements with Heritage Legislation

In Australia, heritage managers are guided by best-practice standards defined in the Burra Charter, first adopted in 1979. The charter is globally admired for its innovative, forward-thinking approach to heritage management. The framers recognized the multivocal and plural contexts of heritage and took steps to ensure fair treatment and sensitivity in determining significance, especially in Indigenous contexts. Although derived in part from the Venice Charter, the Burra Charter departs from emphasizing materiality, monumentality, and aesthetics to recognize instead the transcendent nature of heritage. Although some have critiqued the Burra Charter for its insistence on conservation and stewardship (see, e.g., L. Smith 2004) and reliance on expert knowledge, it honors Aboriginal knowledge and Country in ways that other heritage legislation has not. Flawed or not, the Burra Charter is an evolving and significant document.

While many Australian heritage managers have addressed issues of representation and equality in their practice, recent events bring in to sharp relief the challenges ahead. In June 2014 the government of Western Australia released a draft of the Aboriginal Heritage Amendment Bill 2014. The bill includes amendments to the Aboriginal Heritage Act 1972, which provides for the "preservation on behalf of the community of places and objects" of Traditional Owners. Aboriginal groups and representative bodies, as well as heritage managers, immediately denounced the bill.[13] In fact, in a review of over 150 comments and submissions formally presented to the Parliament on the draft bill, legal scholars and activists found that a majority of submitters were against the bill (Kwaymullina et al. 2015:25). Notwithstanding, the Department of Aboriginal Affairs (DAA) declared that the amendments were critical for supporting industry and development and that "*modest changes* [would] ensure that our Aboriginal heritage can continue to be protected in an efficient and effective way" (emphasis mine).[14] It is true that there is a substantial backlog of sites awaiting assessment. It is also true that Aboriginal groups have sought changes, especially in providing a more culturally sensitive definition of significance (see, e.g., Kwaymullina et al. 2015; Povinelli 2002; L. Smith 2004). But the proposed changes are anything but modest; they align with the needs of industry and the state and would erode Aboriginal rights and protections. Although the draft bill does increase penalties for offenses to destruction of Aboriginal heritage, this is not the same as protecting and representing Aboriginal interests.

If changes proposed are passed, they will have consequences for heritage along the resource frontier. First, the applicant, not the Traditional Owners whose heritage would be adversely affected, has the right of appeal. Second, decision making would be consolidated in one bureaucrat, the chief executive officer (CEO). The CEO will be the sole arbiter in making determinations, removing this role from the Aboriginal Cultural Material Committee (ACMC). Third, the amendment removes the requirement for a specialist (i.e., anthropologist) on the ACMC or that the minister consults with the ACMC. Fourth, the bill would allow permits to be transferred and would be valid in perpetuity. The bill, whether intended or not, repositions who has power in heritage negotiations. In effect, the ACMC will be demoted to an "as needed" advisory role. Without oversight or right of appeal, Traditional Owners will be without clear avenues to voice concerns or protect Country. Some see the bill as a "backwards step for an already outdated Act" (Kwaymullina et al. 2015:25). The Law Society of Western Australia agreed. The impacts may or may not be immediate, but they will be felt deeply. Even so, Aboriginal Affairs minister Peter Collier stated publicly that the amendment would "actually enhance opportunities for Aboriginal people to have a say in what goes on."[15] What opportunities Collier is referring to are not apparent.

Something interesting is happening along the frontier: industry and state needs are driving heritage negotiations and remaking Country. As Victoria Laurie (2014) reported, "the minister [Collier] openly admits that pressure from resource companies and developers is a significant factor in the proposed reforms." Not surprisingly, the Association of Mining and Exploration Companies is a strong supporter of the bill. In these negotiations we see a marked shift toward "industry-friendly site assessment outcomes that has coincided with the appointment of several recent recruits . . . from industry backgrounds" (Bennetts 2015). In an alarming twist, the DAA has recently deregistered twenty-one heritage sites, including the Burrup Peninsula. The sites fall under the new definition of "sacred site" under section 5(a)–(d) of the Aboriginal Heritage Act 1972, which requires physical evidence of religious activity. Because Australia's Supreme Court ruled against the new definition, the sites will likely be placed back on the register. Still, a new era of development-friendly strategies—such as fast-tracking or delisting—is under way. The delisting of the Burrup had almost gone unnoticed until Robin Chapple, a member of the Western Australian Legislative Council, called attention to it and asked for more information about the delisting.

In the remaking of heritage along the frontier, notions of industry, heritage, and Country have converged. Why? First, as John Taylor (2009:65) noted, "much higher proportions of Indigenous people [live] in remote areas," and these areas are often resource rich. Many mines and resource areas are adjacent to or on traditional lands of Indigenous communities (Godden et al. 2008). Second, resource industries often must negotiate with Indigenous groups over cultural heritage and native title (Godden et al. 2008). Although some agreements with Aboriginal communities have provided compensation and avenues for redress, access to wealth and resources is not evenly distributed (see, e.g., Gordon 2011). Third, the definitions of heritage follow anthropological and archaeological criteria (Kwaymullina et al. 2015:26). In the case of the Aboriginal Heritage Act 1972, its anthropological or historical interests would define an Aboriginal heritage landscape. As I have argued, both in chapter 2 and in relation to the New Zealand Maori context, such definitions can eclipse Indigenous systems of knowledge and, more importantly, create obstacles to assert social and political authority. In the case of cultural landscapes we saw how such mobilizations, derived from Western understandings and conceptualizations, tend to collapse complex worldviews and knowledge systems. More importantly, definitions of heritage—or significance—originate outside of Indigenous authority.

The bill is an erosion of heritage protections, and outsiders are, once again, laying claim to Country. Ideas of what constitutes heritage ignore Aboriginal peoples' obligations and responsibilities to care for Country. The amendments, one may argue, bear similarities to earlier assimilation policies that worked to transfer to outsiders the power to own and speak for Aboriginal lands. Settlers, in that case, did not recognize Country, and Traditional Owners were placed at a severe disadvantage. Although Aboriginal legal scholar Peter Dawson (2015:4) hoped that these changes to heritage protections would lessen the "hangover of *terra nullius*," one could argue that the transfer of control over resources and lands is still very much in play. But these changes are also occurring in other ways, and in the next section I draw connections to another form of identity creation occurring along the frontier: corporate heritage discourse (after Weiss 2009).

Corporate Heritage Discourse

In its broadest outlines, corporate heritage discourse refers to the texts, images, and language that are developed by corporate bodies and used to promote corporate activities in and around heritage sites. Corporate heritage discourse and corporate social responsibility (CSR) are not synonymous, but both are strategies that corporations adopt to legitimize activities. CSR refers to the corporate approach of self-regulation and the production of codes of conduct and standards. The broader objective is framed around social and environmental well-being beyond the focus of shareholder profits (Shamir 2004; Welker 2009).[16] CSR initiatives are commonly developed around a corporate conscience or citizenship and framed around a demonstration of a company's commitment to a common good. In mining contexts, for example, companies may draw on CSR initiatives to build connections with communities (Brueckner et al. 2014; Evers et al. 2013; Luning 2012; Rajak 2011; Welker 2009). I make a distinction between corporate discourse or corporate heritage discourse and what Laurajane Smith (2006) calls "authorized heritage discourse." As previously described, Smith (2006:4) argued that a "dominant Western discourse" surrounds heritage that privileges expert knowledge. Although this is clearly the case with corporate mobilizations of heritage, corporate heritage discourse refers to the specific strategies that are developed and created by corporate bodies in relation to heritage. Although there are clearly points of convergence, I want to think here about how corporate discourse creates new protocols and standards around heritage.

For heritage scholars, decentering the discourse and examining how knowledge is produced is a central concern. How, for example, do mining corporations draw on (or create) discourse to legitimize practices? In the South African post-industrial landscape, anthropologist Lindsay Weiss (2014) has shown how the De Beers Mine repackaged colonial legacies into tourism friendly tropes. De Beers sponsored the newly designated Heritage Diamond Route. In return for support, the company receives validation and recognition. But at the same time, the company cloaks its history of conflict, human-rights violations, and environmental impacts within a more neutral and socially acceptable story. De Beers positions the story of its industrial past through the Heritage Route and via the multimillion-dollar museum, hotel, and conference center. On its website, De Beers exclaims that the "Diamond Route grew out of De Beers' century old practice of using its mining-license landholdings for nature conservation purposes."[17] I doubt this is the case. But what is most interesting is how they linked history and heritage in a way that displaces conversations about mining impacts. As Weiss (2014:11) argued, the heritage route "circumvent[s] the sprawling township-scapes populated by former casual laborers, impoverished pensioners and shack-dwellers who continue to live in the shadows of the industrial landscapes." In their enactment of corporate heritage, De Beers not only appropriates the language of sustainability and rights but also washes out the histories and traumas of its industrial past.

But scholars have called attention to the shadow dynamics of industry before (e.g., Kirsch 2014; Sawyer 2004). They have shown how corporate bodies construct discourse to defuse discussion of environmental impacts (see, e.g., Dobrin and Weisser 2002; Goggin 2013; Seagle 2012), authorize and legitimize economic development and nation-building (Rico 2008; Silverman 2011; Winter 2007, 2013), or divert attention away from conflict (Kirsch 2014; Luning 2012; Rajak 2011). Caroline Seagle's (2012) ethnographic exposition of Rio Tinto/QIT Madagascar Mineral's (QMM's) mining practices in Madagascar demonstrated how, through the discourse of sustainability, the company positioned itself as an environmental steward. In constructing discourse through texts and media, the company shifted the focus (and blame) away from impacts from mining and onto local communities and *their* "unsustainable practices." Anthropologist Stuart Kirsch (2014:3) has shown how corporate practices manipulate science and "invoke discourses of sustainability and social responsibility." It is no surprise that Rio Tinto/QMM developed a multimedia campaign that drew from and closely resembled the sustainability imagery of the environmental NGO the World Wildlife Fund (WWF) (Seagle 2012).

Mining companies also promote their interests through discourse and have developed documents, reports, guides, and other literatures. The International Council on Mining and Metals (ICMM), a cohort of mining and metal companies and industries, promotes among its principles the need to "respect cultural heritage of host communities" (ICMM 2012). This admirable and necessary principle is a positive and needed addition to the mining industries lexicon (Akiwumi 2014). ICMM publishes articles, position statements, corporate briefs, and reports that outline and/or address potentially controversial or problematic issues. Their literatures examine issues of sustainable resource development, working with Indigenous peoples, "building capacity," and human rights. ICMM has also developed partnerships with key heritage bodies UNESCO and IUCN, as well as the World Bank and international environmental NGOs such as the WWF (see, e.g., ICMM 2013). In fact, ICMM consulted with IUCN to develop a joint document on mining in World Heritage contexts. The move was promoted as a way to be proactive and respond to the increased encroachment of mining in World Heritage sites (see Coombe and Baird 2015). To be sure, ICMM is also highly informed, and the guides are clearly aimed at influencing opinion and policy. In 2013, for example, ICMM quickly responded to critiques by First Peoples Worldwide concerning ICMM's "Indigenous Peoples and Mining Position Statement." In my reading of ICMM's public response, I thought it circumvented the issue at hand: government and industry relations in Indigenous territories.

Corporate heritage discourse is increasingly used to frame debates and discussions around resource frontiers. I found that in Western Australia, industry (e.g., Rio Tinto, Fortesecue Metals, Woodside LNG, and BHP Billiton) is mobilizing the language of heritage, Indigenous rights, and sustainability in their conceptions of heritage and through their corporate campaigns (Baird 2013; see Figure 6). They draw on the lexicon of environmental or cultural heritage in their negotiations for access to lands and resources. During my research in 2012 and 2014 it was clear that mining companies were tapping into heritage to showcase their activities working with communities. Aboriginal and environmental heritage was promoted on signs, literature, pamphlets, and industry websites. Mining representatives also touched upon heritage in discussions. I am not speculating here about how heritage was mobilized within development discussions or in conversations with Aboriginal groups, but instead calling attention to how cultural heritage is being used as a starting point for discus-

Figure 6. "Thank you Rio Tinto" sign, Dampier, Western Australia, photo by author.

sions. In particular, in the Australian context I found that discourse serves as a framing device that positions industry in largely positive and neutral ways. In Western Australia heritage is de rigueur for discussing relations and responsibilities and part of the social license to conduct business. Aboriginal heritage is invoked in media and public relations, presented at visitor centers, discussed on mine tours, and highlighted in brochures. Woodside's North West Shelf Visitor Centre, for example, draws on Aboriginal Country and heritage to shape visitors' experiences.

And this is the crux of the matter: heritage—and, by way of extension, Coun-try—is being reframed as a resource, one that allows specific histories and sto-ries to be told, stories that are largely celebratory and circumvent discussions about the environmental or social costs of doing business. Think back to the Burrup Peninsula. In the promotion of heritage, contested histories and con-temporary issues are presented as resolved: the corporate heritage discourse sets the agenda, without a space to contest or problematize. Aboriginal owners do have a say in how the area is protected and managed, but at the same time, the majority of the peninsula is retained for industry. What we see is how economic interests and industry needs take precedence over culture and environment. As I have argued elsewhere (Baird 2013), I suspect that the heritage discourse is deflecting other conversations such as whether industry is compatible with environmental or social sustainability. Instead, I see the conversations focus-ing more on celebrating heritage, without grappling with the impacts of how heritage is destroyed or damaged in industrial contexts. At the same time, the huge industrial estate on the environmentally sensitive peninsula, as well as the impacts of industry on local communities, is excised from the discussion.

The Murujuga Management Plan, described earlier, is part of the larger cor-pus of reports, working documents, and management plans that can be viewed as negotiation documents. These documents are often the starting point for conversations between local communities and mining corporations. Although not always identified as such, these discussions are central to cultural or natu-ral heritage. At the Porgera Mine in Papua New Guinea, anthropologist Alex Golub (2014) showed how negotiations between the Indigenous Ipili and Placer Dome were mediated through the development of the Porgera Mine Sustain-ability Report. The report was the result of nearly two years of negotiations that, Golub (2014:24) argued, were "condensed into a single, authoritative, and anon-ymously voiced narrative." The importance of the twenty-page booklet cannot be underestimated: it served as a guide to operations and the environmental and social future of the valley, and it was used and circulated in all negotiations. In effect, the report works to depoliticize negotiations.

Corporate discourse also draws on and creates historical myths. The politics and economics of mining in the Upper Peninsula (UP) of Michigan, described in the last chapter, provides a compelling example. A resurgence of mining in the region brought the promise of stability through an infusion of money into the depressed economy. Eagle Mine, originally developed by Kennecott, a sub-sidiary of Rio Tinto, now owned by Lundin Mining Corporation of Toronto, is an underground, high-quality nickel mine. At the onset, the mine has emboldened serious objections over sacred sites, groundwater discharge, and what some see as the softening of environmental regulations. The biggest environmental threat is related to sulfide mining and its potential to create irreversible impacts on wetlands in the Lake Superior Watershed. But the mine is also sited on Eagle Rock, an Ojibwa sacred site. In the time leading up to the opening of the mine, Kennecott representatives promoted the mine's role in job creation. Rio Tinto sent representatives, held town meetings, and seemed interested in what the community had to say, promoting the idea that "Your community is our community."[18] At the same time, the Keweenaw Bay Indian Community called out social and environmental impacts, especially the mine's wastewater discharges and Michigan Department of Environmental Quality's (MDEQ) new ideas of mitigation. The complicated discussions involve MDEQ reports, mining permits, proposals, and public review. Nevertheless, despite real evidence of the issues with acid water drainage, the MDEQ granted a permit in 2007 and the State of Michigan passed new mining regulations that weakened environmental water protections. The debate continues, and new mining projects are announced regularly.

But what is important to this discussion is how the campaign to promote the mine drew on the region's industrial heritage. Rio Tinto and, later, Lundin position themselves as a paternal presence, bringing care and concern for jobs to the region. They promoted the history of mining in the region, which served as a touchstone for discussions. Not only does this help these companies' causes, but it also draws attention away from opposition and contestation. Today, Lundin supports the development of the Iron Ore Heritage Trail and regularly supports the well-developed heritage industry in the UP. But the UP is not an anomaly: the rhetoric of economic development is seen along other resource frontiers, such as forestry, bioprospecting, and seabed mining, and new areas opened up by climate change that intersect with heritage. In Utah, Alton Coal Development Company proposes to mine nearly fifty million tons of coal from a site only ten miles from Bryce Canyon in Utah. The discourse maps onto the rhetoric—and real need—for jobs for the community. In this case, the National Park Service and Fish and Wildlife Service have recommended that the Department of the Interior reject the coal lease, and tribal communities are actively opposing the mine.[19]

Without any doubt, discourse significantly shapes and influences debates. In heritage contexts, extractive industries are funding, producing, and disseminating knowledge. They also fund academic research, work with government and international heritage agencies, develop and distribute white papers, and promote their activities through social media. And while it is true that these corporate bodies are taking steps to be proactive and work with descendant communities, there may be another possibility, namely, that by taking the lead, industry is framing the contexts of their mining interests at heritage sites. By mapping the contours of the debate, industry can promote its agenda and be a key knowledge generator. From this perspective, the changes in heritage legislation and the ascendency of corporate discourse provide indicators of what is to come.

The project of deconstructing corporate discourse has its challenges. Clearly, extractive industries are easy targets. And as engineering students at the university where I teach remind me, these industries provide jobs and resources. Nevertheless, although opinions will vary widely, scholars need to explore the evolving intersections between heritage and industry and how industry shapes policy around heritage. Aboriginal scholar Marcia Langton (2012, 2013) argues that participation in the mining economy is the way toward poverty reduction and transforming Indigenous communities (see also Langton and Longbottom 2012). This is a different issue than the one I am describing here.

What I am pointing to is how discourse obscures power by limiting the discursive space and restricting forums for debate. Corporate discourse presents its vision of engagement and promotes its version of events. It focuses the message and discloses only information that serves its purpose: to persuade. Heritage is presented in ahistorical and apolitical ways, and what is washed out are issues of contested pasts and presents, land-rights claims, and environmental contexts. Corporate discourse directs the conversation toward what a company deems relevant, while at the same time bridging away from contested pasts or contemporary concerns. Lundin Mining promotes the Iron Ore Heritage route in Michigan, devoid of discussions about whose "heritage is our history." If it did address these issues, Lundin or Woodside, for example, would have to discuss the vocal and active opposition to their activities. But there is a much more disturbing possibility, namely, that heritage is taken up by industry and that in the reframing, nostalgic visions obscure the real histories and potential inequalities at play. Corporate discourse becomes a medium for presenting history, without discomfort and with its version of events: heritage is performed, and industry is exempt from responsibility. In fact, the very real environmental issues that mining and industry bring to communities are not even up for discussion.

Knowledge *of* Country

But for all the promises and promotions, the Pilbara region has been struggling. In April 2015, iron ore prices hit their lowest point, from a high in 2008, forcing a reconsideration of the proposed benefits. The falling demand of iron ore, attributed to a slowdown in China's economic building surge, has had far-reaching impacts. To address the loss of revenue, the Australian government announced that it would pursue "structural savings," that is, cuts to health and welfare. At the same time, mining giants Rio Tinto and BHP Billiton have consistently refused to slow production, while simultaneously proposing spending and job cuts. Across the region, smaller resource companies struggle to compete and some have dropped out of production.

Even communities that benefited from the rush have failed. The newly declared city of Karratha transformed itself from a small mining community into a key industry player, emboldened by a seemingly inexhaustible infusion of development dollars from funding via Australia's Pilbara Cities initiative and Royalties for Regions. The city grew with revenue from new businesses and a higher tax base, as well as the workforce that constructed Woodside's LNG plant. Today the "cosmopolitan" city struggles with its new identity. While Woodside boasted it generated fifteen thousand new jobs, and according to its website "made a significant contribution to Western Australian and Australian economies," the shift from construction to production in 2012 was felt widely: housing prices collapsed, businesses shuttered, and town managers scrambled to recruit new industries. In March 2015, *Mining Weekly* reported that Woodside would make further adjustments (i.e., cuts) to "address the impacts in the commodities market" (Swanepoel 2015). Mayor of Karratha Peter Long noted "we are a resource town and Western Australia really is a resource state, so when the industry pulls back we all suffer" (Spriggs and Bell 2015). What this means in the long term is still not clear.

What is clear is that the Pilbara region's red dirt, fringing coral reefs and beaches, small towns and remote Aboriginal communities, do not exist in isolation. They connect to powerful steelmaking companies in China, the boardrooms and offices of mining companies, and the stock exchanges in London and Sydney. The economies of the Pilbara rise and fall with the sale and speculation of minerals and gas. When I returned to the Pilbara in 2016 there were signs of stress everywhere. Sales of homes remain well below peak levels, and foreclosures reached their most critical level in 2016. Despite this, townspeople I interviewed in Dampier, Karratha, and Onslow mostly remained hopeful. While they spoke of worries about jobs and debt obligations, they also spoke in terms of "potential" and "possibilities." As one former mining engineer, laid off from a round of job cuts, explained to me, "The economy will rebound, and the jobs will too."

What is at stake along the resource frontiers of Western Australia? Mining and development increasingly shapes heritage and Country: Marandoo mine, the industrial estate on the Burrup, and Western Australia's newest domestic gas and LNG plant—Wheatstone Project in Onslow on Thalanyji Country. Onslow today is a literal boomtown. During my visit in 2012, the town was still in the early stages of construction. Chevron invested nearly $20 billion to develop the megaproject. By the time I returned in 2014 and again in 2016, the community had had an opportunity to think through the changes they were experiencing. The community shared their concerns and also support for the project. Yet, many feared what was happening in their once-quiet fishing community. People I talked with at the newly renovated local caravan park, some of whom have been going there for twenty years—were angry about the impacts of dredging on essential fish habitats. They told me that the fishing spots they have fished for years, as well as the nearshore habitats, were ruined, and they had to spend more money on gas to boat further out. Although Chevron earmarked $10 million to mediate environmental offsets (i.e., damage to marine fauna and fringing coral reefs), the impacts to the region's environmental and cultural heritage are considerable. It was almost as if people were still stunned by just how fast these changes came and how they didn't quite match up to their expectations (i.e., economic development and revitalization).

In what ways is heritage mobilized as a political resource? In the Pilbara something extraordinary is taking place—a rush, in a way, a fervent push for development. At the same time, there is a clash between ideologies and ideas. A simplistic view would be that the debate is over the seemingly ravenous appetites for mineral wealth or the pursuit of profit. And perhaps this is part of the issue. But it is also about how Country is changed in the process. What I am arguing here is that part of that work is done through corporate discourse. Think about the work discourse does: it contains, it manages, it packages heritage in nostalgic, ahistorical, and apolitical ways. It presents its view of good governance and good relations in a way that ignores systemic issues of violence, erasures of history, and environmental impacts. It presents these issues as resolved. What part of these histories or of these stories are we missing? What is lost in the making of the frontier? How are company strategies and practices mapping onto discourse and practice? This is what new heritage landscapes encompass: borders redefined, landscapes reimagined, growth and investment, exploitation and divestment, heritage that is in service to the state. These landscapes are part of a new order of things. Tracing the multiple and complex rules of engagement is urgent. How do negotiations within these new heritage landscapes provide the blueprint for negotiations in other contexts?

Arriving at answers to these questions requires clarifying the competing claims and tracing the varied agendas of global institutions, corporations, the nation-state, and stakeholders. How do corporate conceptions of heritage intersect with ideas and issues surrounding land and access, indigeneity, sustainable development, and the rights of Indigenous peoples? In the Western Australian context, we saw how governments have been supportive in developing the region's industry, while at the same time promoting the area's heritage along the resource frontier. I made this point to show that the heritage landscapes of Western Australia do not exist in isolation; the architecture and strategies are found in other contexts. Take for example the U.S. Department of State's announcement in 2014 of plans to support the New Silk Road. The road provides the infrastructure and the political architecture to open regional energy markets, reduce barriers to trade, and support international development in Asia. In response, China's president, Xi Jinping, announced his plans for the New Silk Road project—a multibillion-dollar initiative. The architects map modern infrastructure—pipelines, high-speed rail, roads, and ports—onto the history and heritage of the ancient networks of trade and industry that once stretched from eastern Asia to the Mediterranean (*Economist* 2014). Something important is happening here, a translation of sorts. The ancient Silk Road, and its connections to the people, landscapes, and the past, has been reimagined as a technological highway. That is, much like the Pilbara example, the past is in service to development and geopolitical agendas, especially in connecting to remote territories and their natural resources. The questions remain: How are rights and resources negotiated along the frontier? What are the impacts of capitalist relations (Barney 2009), the role of state power (Kirsch 2014), or the intersections with transnational conservation industries (Goldman 2005; Greenough and Tsing 2003; Neumann 1998) along the frontier? How exactly is heritage and the language of Indigenous rights being used in claim-making, and how do actors work within these "new heritage landscapes"?

6

Toward a Critical Theory of Heritage

Law and culture never change. You can do what you like to this land,
but whatever you do, this land never change. They think you can do
anything with it . . . but in the end maybe this land might turn on us.
One day he got to turn on us.

Kurrama elder, Karijini National Park, Western Australia

Karijini National Park, Western Australia, July 2014

We are standing just below the summit of Mount Bruce in Karijini National
Park—known as Punurrunha to the Traditional Owners of these lands, the
Banyjima, Kurrama, and Innawonga Aboriginal people (see Figure 7). We had
hiked up in the early-morning hours, navigating its steep western face, in hopes
of getting a better view and some pictures of Rio Tinto's Marandoo mine.[1] Australians tend to have an optimistic view of people's hiking abilities (and courage),
as the trail was marked as Class 3, though its dizzying drop-offs and slippery
terrain seemed to me more like a Class 5. We had spent two weeks exploring
Karijini's gorges and plains and walking on Country with Aboriginal Rangers—and as luck would have it, talking at length with mine workers on holiday
who camped near us for four days. There really is no way to adequately capture
the beauty and starkness of this place: deep gorges and pools, yellow-flowering
cassias and red kangaroos, termite mounds and mulga trees, and banded iron
formations that geologists say are more than two billion years old. As I looked
toward Marandoo Hill, I could see an iron ore train heading toward the port of
Dampier on the privately owned Hamersley Iron Ore Railway. Although I had
talked with many people about the mine during our visit, it was still jarring to
see an active mine in this place.[2]

To know Country, you need to know its stories. And while I did come to
know a few of these, this is not the same as knowledge *of* Country. I do know
that it must be tended to and respected, and that it connects people to their

Figure 7. Karijini National Park Visitor Centre, Australia, photo by author.

world and to others (including plants and animals, water and rocks). I also know that such places and stories serve as touchstones to culture and deep knowledge that is far beyond what I could describe. I have often thought that these places may hold the antidote to many of our societal and environmental problems. I do not mean this in a nostalgic or romantic sense that imparts mystical or otherworldly properties to the landscape, but one that recognizes that Law and protocol, and stories and knowledge are trusted systems that are passed down through generations to maintain the land, guide behavior, and ensure cultural and ecological well-being. As the epigraph to this chapter is meant to illustrate, these systems of knowledge are durable. As the Kurrama elder stated, "Law and culture never change." His words are a testament to the resilience of Country, despite violence, negation, misinterpretation, and regulation; they serve to re-inforce the centrality of Law and culture. But at the same time, he intimates that the compact between people and land could erode in ways that are irrevocable. "In the end," he warns, "maybe this land might turn on us. One day he got to turn on us."

As I have argued throughout this book, landscapes matter. They exist be-yond places on a map; they are how communities articulate their identities and their relationships to the world. Landscapes are mapped and sung, lived and contested, walked on and turned over, cared for and held. But at the same time, landscapes are sites of negotiations; they are constrained and contested, and me-diated within systems of exclusion and oppression. We know that landscapes are imbricated in nation-building and tourism schema, as well as sustainability and poverty-reduction initiatives. Raising the question of how to make sense of the points of connection, to make these ethnographically visible, one would have to think about the politics of making place. Do we merely reckon with the "on the ground traces of places that have been destroyed" (Gordillo 2014:11)? I would say, instead, that we need to rethink the very nature of such engagements, that is, to think through the political dynamics, cultural processes, and frictions to better understand the powerful work that heritage does (after Tsing 2005).

Thus, the central thesis of this book is that it is essential to locate the socio-political and historical contexts of our work. Understanding these will extend our understanding of where, for example, colonial structures remain in heritage practices and how these are regulated, reproduced, and maintained. As the ex-ample of Uluru–Kata Tjuta National Park, a sacred Aboriginal landscape man-aged in collaboration with the Anangu, meant to show, the histories of land alienation and violence were occluded in narratives of the park. That is, the legacies of colonial policies were embedded in how the site was managed. It is clear that many of these debates and tensions are rooted in the control of Coun-try. Land alienation and dispossession at Uluru, as well as the Pilbara, could be read as a form of structural violence, one where the "system builds and rebuilds itself, neutralizing and absorbing opposition and reform" (Kirmayer 2004:321). The system, in this case, can be traced back to the doctrine of *terra nullius*, which transferred the power to own and speak for Aboriginal lands to European colonists and made it easier for them to impose their ideas of land use and land ownership. The modern vestiges of this all-encompassing ideology are in full bloom in the negotiations around Country, where ideas of Country put forward by industry are imposed and, in many cases, Aboriginal peoples' obligations are ignored.

One could argue that such histories are not central to current management policies and practices. But as I have argued throughout this book, refusal to address these histories in any meaningful way has consequences for stakeholder communities. If these are presented in abstraction, then fighting to reclaim lands or to protect cultural and intellectual heritage rights makes resistance or opposition seem unwarranted. As I see it, we must include these painful histories—of subordination, oppression, and dispossession—if only to bring clarity and context to contemporary struggles for land rights and recognition. How history is told has consequence and often serves the interests of those in power. Opening up the analyses to understand whose perspectives are privileged and whose voices are excluded will go a long way to recognizing systems of dominance and subordination.

As the examples in this book demonstrated, landscapes are central to the business of heritage. While a full appraisal of these contexts was not possible, it is important to note that the business of heritage extends well beyond tourist and recreational venues. Heritage is a global industry that is central to and intersects with the interests of nation-states, government agencies, corporations, philanthropic organizations, and NGOs. As such, experts are central to this work. They shape and broker ideas of heritage, provide technical and policy advice, inform decision makers, and mediate boundary disputes. Increasingly, nation-states employ experts and partner with heritage agencies, which, in some ways, works to minimize or distract attention from their ideological positions and political motivations. More and more, we see how heritage expertise is deployed beyond the traditional heritage remit and taken up by private, corporate, and industry interests. This is certainly true with the increasing centrality of extractive activities in heritage contexts, as we saw in the Western Australian examples. We also know that many of these activities are mediated and sanctioned through laws, policies, and practices. The proposed weakening of amendments to the Aboriginal Heritage Act 1972 to allow for more industry-friendly site assessment comes at a cost. To understand heritage in this way allows for a recognition of how experts, agencies, institutions, and practitioners influence and shape policy issues at local, national, and international levels. There are many benefits in recognizing these contexts, as nation-building often begins and ends with land, and understanding how nation-states promote heritage landscapes for their heritage values to national and international audiences can go a long way in understanding their motivations, especially in cases where traditional territories are promoted as tourist destinations and/or economic resources, that is, when other people's heritage is marked and sold as a resource of national identity.

As scientists and others today debate whether or not we have entered into a new human age, heritage scholars rightfully ask how heritage should be defined in these contexts (Solli et al. 2011). Termed the Anthropocene, from the Greek *Anthropo*, the proposed geological epoch references human-caused changes in environments as well as their consequences. Whether the date of inscription begins with the origins of agriculture or the Industrial Revolution is largely semantics. What is important is that the Anthropocene, or Donna Haraway's (2016) preferred conceptualization, Cthulucene, is defined not by geology but by human action and choice, as much as by acidified oceans, animal extinctions, and "carbon dioxide concentrations [at levels] . . . not seen in 400,000 years" (Monastersky 2015:145). Clearly, heritage landscapes—industrial, archaeological, urban, and Indigenous—should figure prominently in these discussions. These are the contexts in which we will see tensions over land and resources, but also the sites where we will be addressing environmental sustainability, climate change, and resource depletion, among other issues. Whether it is Native Alaskan communities that were devastated by the *Exxon Valdez* oil spill, or Aboriginal communities mediating intensive resource projects on Country, we see how landscapes are essential zones of contestation. Our work will be important to making clear the different actors and players—from Native-owned corporations, to those who work with industry and land-management agencies, or corporate bodies negotiating interests through heritage—and how these are mediated and for whom.

A significant argument I have made in this book is that although scholars have clearly grappled with the varied political and social contexts of heritage, how to address these contexts *in* our work is not as clear. Yet, I am also not entirely sure of the best approach to do this. Without a doubt, there needs to be space within our discussions in reports, nominations, publications, and presentations, because if not, they exist in isolation of larger mediating contexts. But at the same time, I cannot help but think that engagements with landscapes could include emancipatory discourse and/or be deployed in ways that mobilize agency. In many cases, heritage professionals work to protect the intellectual and property rights of descendant communities in heritage initiatives. To make these protections stronger, I see developing research protocols, in collaboration with descendant and stakeholder communities, that take on the political and historical contexts and consider issues of confidentiality, intellectual property rights, access, right of review, and ownership of data—that is, providing a tangible way to bring in the controversial topics and concerns. As I see it, to develop dialogue and expand the context for this type of knowledge in heritage and environmental management practices, we must restructure how we report our work and the laws and practices that guide our investigations.

Yet, despite weighing in on these issues, heritage scholars have also been marginalized in discussions (see Solli et al. 2011). It is not clear if this is because of the ascendancy of environmentally focused initiatives, such as ecosystems services and natural capital, both of which have been critiqued for not prioritizing culture (see, e.g., Milcu et al. 2013), or because heritage is viewed as an adjunct or not essential to these discussions. Whatever the case, it is essential that heritage take a more prominent position in these debates. As extractive activities increase across the globe, new areas are opened up for development, and environmental disasters become more common, it becomes even more urgent that heritage be put on the agenda. After all, many of these resource-rich areas and sites of disasters map onto ancestral lands or places of importance to Indigenous or descendant communities. As we saw in the case of Western Australia and Mongolia, these activities and environmental initiatives work in ways that decontextualize connections and/or transfer ownership of lands. Clearly, it is critical that we know the mechanisms through which competing claims are made and varied agendas advanced.

A note on what this book is not. It is not a critique of heritage scholars or professionals. And I underline this point. At first read, it may seem that the argument stacks up against heritage scholars, that somehow they have been negligent or had failed to understand how heritage landscapes and politics are inextricably linked. But, the argument I make in this book—that heritage landscapes must be considered within their sociohistorical contexts—is not focused on individuals, but instead the logic that underlies negotiations. By shifting the focus away from individuals or surface tensions, I hope we can take a closer look at the source of those tensions: the structures that support and create inequalities. This would mean investigating how epistemologies of landscapes intersect with power, identity, and the construction of knowledge. That would mean understanding that our models, theories, and practices of heritage work through systems of power and exclusion. That is, as I have argued throughout, to understand the social and political implications of landscapes *as* heritage.

This book is not an attack on extractive industries. It is a discussion of how their activities intersect with heritage. As I aimed to show, landscapes are central to the *business* of heritage. As described, heritage is a global industry with wide range and reach. I have tried to show that industries shape and frame ideas of heritage through corporate initiatives and discourses, and in ways that have not been fully acknowledged. While it is true that mining companies have implemented proactive approaches, increased Indigenous participation, and promoted socially responsible mining practices, it is also true that these approaches vary depending on location and that tensions exist around heritage in mining-affected communities. From management practices that view water as a resource, overlooking how water is integral to Aboriginal Country, to heated debates over the siting of an industrial estate and mega-LNG plant on a landscape rich with cultural heritage, we see how heritage is transmuted in the process. That is, heritage is reframed as a resource. As I see it, the job of the critical heritage theorist is to ask questions and examine contradictions, even at the risk of overstating these contradictions.

And this is not the time to relax our examinations: multinational extractive corporations yield considerable power and are influencing changes in heritage legislation. What is new is how heritage expertise is deployed beyond traditional contexts and now serves the needs of development, nation-state, industry, and other projects. After all, if one compares the reach and influence of a transnational mining corporation to that of Traditional Owners, it is evident that power is asymmetrical and a mediating component in these relationships.

In thinking through what we can do, what is most needed are multi-sited studies that trace the logics of heritage landscapes in all of their complexity. The "After Oil: Transitioning to a New World of Energy" project provides some insights into how interdisciplinary partnerships and approaches can be used to address social, cultural and political changes.[3] The focus is on locating political structures, cultural dynamics, and values and beliefs that intersect with seemingly unrelated energy contexts. In this way, the collaborators have repositioned the questions to show the shape and force of energy and oil. This can be illustrative for heritage landscapes. How, for example, do resource industries conduct business and use heritage in different contexts or continents? Are there differences in heritage management in the Global North and South? How can understanding these variances and local contexts help us to institutionalize consultation and shift from experts to communities? One idea is to change the way we report our findings, or present our nominations to heritage agencies. Another is to expand the significance component to also include the politics of the site, ongoing land claims, and other issues. More importantly, it is critical that we remove the nostalgic lens that so many of these sites are viewed with. The Copper Country that I now call home is steeped in sentimentality that works as a stranglehold for a real consideration of the health and well-being of the community. We must work to remove the patina of place and "romanticized ruin" and to take on the histories of violence and exclusion, environmental concerns, and grief that remain after the industries have gone (after Gordillo 2014).

And this is where I see the field of critical heritage theory having its greatest contribution to make. It has enormous potential to shift the conversation away from critiques of shortcomings to instead provide recommendations—a new engagement with heritage landscapes that makes room for multiple understandings and brings in subjugated and stakeholder knowledge. This is where the work of making sense comes into play—of fleshing out the rules of engagement. The key is in tracing specific strategies and tying these to corresponding practices or specific historical moments. This is where comparative and critical ethnographic approaches will be most useful, by tracking how strategies and practices are mapping onto heritage discourse to help to capture how heritage is taken up and deployed by global bodies, industry, and others. By seeing heritage landscapes in this way, we can see where our practices intersect with power, identity, and the construction of knowledge, and recognize how the personal intersects with the political.

Epilogue

The "City" of Karratha, Western Australia, 2016

I am back in Western Australia. It has been only two years since I visited this home on Crockett Way in Karratha. I park the van in front of what had once been a well-kept home. I've come to see if my former informant is still living there; I had lost track of him after he was laid off in 2014. I assume he has moved away and that his home is in foreclosure. I base this solely on anecdotal evidence: a broken window, a yard overgrown with weeds, and a for sale sign that appears to have been there for some time. I hear a dog barking and see someone peek out from the home next door, signs that not all the workers have moved away.

It is hard to reconcile this place—what used to be called the "Powerhouse of the Pilbara"—with the place I see now. The once small mining community set its sights high, aiming to be a key industry player (see Figure 8). Life in the city is clearly different today. With industry waning, the region no longer benefits from the revenue, or the infusions of cash from government. Gone are the influx of moneyed workers, in their fluorescent "hi-vis" clothing and the fly-in/fly-out workers that drove housing costs well beyond what is expected in more cosmopolitan cities. The grocery store is not well stocked. Many of the restaurants and stores are shuttered. And, my conversations with community members are different now, punctuated with long silences. People are worried and have difficulty imagining the future. I read in the margins of my notes the word *riptide*—I don't remember writing this, but I guess it is meant to indicate the sense that he was fighting to stay in place, when perhaps the better approach would be to let go.

What is clear is that the fortunes of the Pilbara rise and fall with the sale and speculation of minerals and gas. Many bought into the promise of steady economic growth, and the idea that the region's natural resources are inexhaustible, that these alone can sustain the community. The events of the Pilbara—its

Figure 8. City center, Karratha, Western Australia, photo by author.

boom-and-bust cycles, its newly declared city, its shifting economies—domi-
nate the discussions. Yet, economies recover (or not); businesses rebuild (or
don't). What troubles me is that our discussions have overlooked the changes
to land, to the environment, and to Country. I am reminded of a passage from
Cormac McCarthy's *The Crossing* (1995:148), where the priest prophesies that
the "passing of armies and the passing of sands in the desert are one. There is
no favoring," meaning no justice, no merit, but an inevitable "reckoning whose

ledgers would be drawn up and dated" (1995:5). Whether the economies of the Pilbara will recover, the changes to the land and Country cannot be undone. In what ways will we lament the loss of this land? How can this fragile and stunningly beautiful place repair? These questions demand our attention, something beyond reductive attempts and explanations: to recognize that our actions have consequences, whether we take notice or not.

Appendix

Chronology of Events Related to Uluṟu–Kata Tjuṯa

1872 First European explorer visits Uluṟu.

1873 Explorer W. C. Gosse climbs Uluṟu and renames it Ayers Rock.

1920 Northern Territory establishes the Petermann Aboriginal Reserve under the Northern Territory Crown Lands Ordinance.

1944 The first organized tourist group visits Ayers Rock.

1958 The Ayers Rock–Mount Olga area is excised from Petermann Reserve and designated Ayers Rock–Mount Olga National Park.

1959 Park managers build an airstrip and non-Aboriginal residences and discourage Aṉangu from visiting the park.

1963 Former park ranger Bill Harney publishes *To Ayers Rock and Beyond*.

1965 Anthropologist Charles Pearce Mountford publishes *Ayers Rock: Its People, Their Beliefs, and Their Art*.

1966 A chain is installed onto the rock face of Uluṟu to assist climbers.

1972 The Ininti Store is built and leased to the Aṉangu community.

1973 The Commonwealth recommends management rights for Aṉangu owners.
      Aṉangu members form the Uluṟu Community, later called the Mutitjulu Community.

1974 The first Aṉangu sacred site is fenced.

1976 The safety chain on Uluṟu is extended to the summit.

1977 Uluṟu–Kata Tjuṯa becomes a Commonwealth National Park under the National Parks and Wildlife Conservation Act.
      The park is designated a Biosphere Reserve under the UNESCO Man and Biosphere Programme.
      The park is listed on the Register of the National Estate under the Australian Heritage Commission Act.
      Ownership of the park is transferred to the director of the National Parks and Wildlife Service, preventing Aṉangu Traditional Owners from claiming Uluṟu under the Aboriginal Land Rights (Northern Territory) Act (ALRA).

1979 The Uluru (Ayers Rock) National Park and Lake Amadeus/Luritja Land Claim is filed under ALRA, but the Commonwealth denies the claim.

1983 The village of Yulara is built outside park boundaries. After completion, the number of visitors to the park doubles to 80,000 per year.

    The Commonwealth amends ALRA to return the title of Uluru–Kata Tjuta National Park to the Traditional Owners. The title is not granted until 1985.

1985 October 21: sixteen hectares are added to park.

    October 26: the governor gives the titled deeds of the park to Anangu owners, who immediately lease the park to the director of National Parks and Wildlife Service for a 99-year term.

    December 10: first Joint Management Board is established.

1986 A Board of Management with an Aboriginal majority is established.

    Management of the park is turned over to the Australian National Parks and Wildlife Service.

    Anthropologist Robert Layton publishes *Uluru: An Aboriginal History of Ayers Rock*.

1987 The park is listed as a natural site on the World Heritage list under criteria (vii) and (ix).

1993 The official name of the park is changed to Uluru–Kata Tjuta National Park.

1994 Uluru is listed as a cultural landscape on the World Heritage list under criteria (v) and (vi).

1995 Anangu Tours Party Ltd., an Anangu-owned firm, is established to conduct tours in the park.

1997 Workshops are held with Anangu, park staff, and other organizations to incorporate Anangu values and views into the Park Plan of Management.

    Traditional Owners for the Yulara town site file a native title claim with the National Native Title Tribunal.

2000 The Sydney Olympics torch relay begins at Uluru–Kata Tjuta, bringing international attention to the park.

    The Uluru–Kata Tjuta Board of Management and the director of National Parks submit the Fourth Plan of Management.

2001 The Uluru climb is closed for three weeks to mark the death of an important Anangu elder. The decision is criticized by many, including Northern Territory.

2009 The draft of the Fifth Plan of Management is presented by the Uluṟu–Kata Tjuṯa Board of Management and the director of National Parks for public comment.

Notes

Prologue

1. Anthropologist Deborah Bird Rose (1996:1) has described *Country* as "nourishing terrain," a useful metaphor that offers a way to connect a multitude of concepts that reference Aboriginal knowledge systems, lifeways, and relationships to land, events, people, ancestors, plants, animals, places, and so on.

Chapter 1. Landscapes *as* Heritage

1. The terms *cultural landscapes* and *heritage landscapes* are often used interchangeably. To maintain the distinction, I use the term *heritage landscapes* to place attention on the sociohistorical contexts.

2. As this book went to production, the Oceti Skowin Oyate (the Great Sioux Nation), the Standing Rock Sioux Tribe, and many other Indigenous nations were actively protesting against the siting of the Dakota Access Pipeline. Although many media reports emphasize the environmental issues related to the protest, the tribes attempted to leverage heritage legislation, including the National Historic Preservation Act and Section 106 responsibilities, to argue for their rights and the protection of cultural landscapes and resources. They were not successful.

3. Although scholars had used the term *critical heritage studies* before, at the time of my dissertation work in 2007 its full potential had not yet been explored. To be clear, it is not that these types of studies were not undertaken: Rodney Harrison (2010) had conceptualized the term in a series of courses, and Lisa Breglia (2006) deployed it in her study of the politics of heritage in Mexico.

4. It is important to note that critical heritage departs from what Laurajane Smith (2006) and others (Carman 2000; Harvey 2001) refer to as "heritage studies." This is an important distinction. Carman (2000) notes that some archaeologists may not view themselves as heritage scholars but rather view heritage studies as related to the fields of museum and tourism studies. This is surprising, because much of the work that archaeologists do relates to heritage practices: significance and impact assessment; survey, evaluation, and mitigation; and traditional cultural properties assessments. Although heritage studies are also interdisciplinary, they focus on "modern practices of conservation, tourism, and museums and site visitation" (L. Smith 2006:2) and, in some cases, tend to be apolitical in their approaches. It is not that heritage scholars do not offer critiques, but instead that they are often concerned with (and constrained by) the management of heritage from institutional perspectives. In

such contexts, there is less room to address how heritage plays out in the larger sociopolitical sphere.

5. Swedish geographer Mats Widgren (2010) provides a brief and useful overview of the intellectual history of the modern school of cultural landscape research (see also Olwig 1996).

6. Still, by the 1960s, ideological differences between scientific and humanistic approaches in geography caused scholars to split: scientific modes of investigation encompassed a strongly positivist slant, with the objective of documenting and evaluating humans in physical space, whereas humanist approaches were committed to understanding human experience (Anschuetz et al. 2001; Olwig 1996, 2004). Of course, this dividing line is not unique to geography and can be seen in the disciplines of archaeology, history, and anthropology.

7. Two terms that deserve mention—*place* and *space*—are fundamental to the study of landscapes. Scholars examine how people form relationships with the landscapes they live in and move through, how they attach meanings to spaces to create places, and how the experiences of living in those places shape their meanings and practices (e.g., Basso 1996; Heidegger 1977; Ingold 1993, 2000). As the geographer Yi-Fu Tuan (1977:6) noted, place is central to discussions of experience: "We live, act and orient ourselves in a world that is richly and profoundly differentiated into places, yet at the same time we seem to have a meager understanding of . . . the ways in which we experience them."

8. Places have broad appeal to anthropologists and social scientists, more generally. For examples see Basso 1996; Casey 1996; Giddens 1984; Ingold 1995; and Low and Lawrence-Zúñiga 2003.

Chapter 2. The Politics of Place: Uluru–Kata Tjuṯa National Park, Australia

1. See http://samemory.sa.gov.au/site/page.cfm?c=7213&mode=singleImage, accessed December 15, 2016.

2. Under the lease, the park's Board of Management is composed of six Aṉangu representatives (equally represented by men and women), the director of national parks, and representatives from Northern Territory, the tourism industry, and the environmental community. Parks Australia compensates Aṉangu a portion of revenues and an annual rent price. Many members of the Aṉangu community work in the park as service providers, guides, or staff workers. The park manager, who acts on behalf of the director, manages day-to-day responsibilities. The EPBC Act requires that a Plan of Management be filed every seven years, although this was changed in the 2009 Plan of Management.

3. See http://www.theguardian.com/world/2013/jul/09/people-still-climbing-uluru-closure, accessed December 16, 2016.

4. Transcripts of this interview can be found at http://pmtranscripts.pmc.gov.au/release/transcript-16678, accessed January 4, 2017.

5. More can be found at http://www.abc.net.au/pm/content/2008/s2620549.htm, accessed December 16, 2016.

6. See http://whc.unesco.org/archive/repbu94a.htm, accessed December 16, 2016.

7. See http://whc.unesco.org/en/list/447, accessed January 2, 2017.

8. Name suppressed, October 13, 1989, Letter to Secretariat, World Heritage Committee, Box 77, World Heritage Centre Archives, Paris.

9. Some New Age practitioners believe Uluru–Kata Tjuta to be one of Earth's chakras (see, e.g., http://www.rainbowserpent.co.uk, accessed August 27, 2014). At comparable heritage sites—Stonehenge, in Britain, and Mato Tipila, or Devil's Tower, in North Dakota—New Age practitioners and various stakeholders (land managers, Indigenous groups, visitors) come into conflict about use, access, and interpretation of these sites.

Chapter 3. Of Environments and Landscapes

1. While a doctoral student I created the Alaskan Rock Art Database to facilitate data management and analysis of site-specific information from pictograph and petroglyph sites throughout Alaska. Because of my knowledge of Alaskan rock art, I was invited to participate in the Kosciusko and Heritage Expedition by the Forest Service archaeologist for the Prince of Wales Island Ranger Districts, Terry Fifield, and the Kosciusko Island Rock Art Project leaders Dr. James Keyser and George Poetshat. Sealaska Corporation provided permission to visit a historic cemetery site and provided volunteers to oversee the investigations. The Heritage Expedition was developed in partnership with a private company, Alaska Sea Adventures, and aimed to provide chartered guests an opportunity to assist with an archaeological research project while also learning of the region's cultural and natural history.

2. As a former resident of Oregon, I was familiar with and accustomed to the logging industry. I was not naive about the U.S.D.A. Forest Service's mission related to resource extraction, but the extent and amount of logging on the island was staggering.

3. The Sealaska Heritage Institute is sponsored by the Sealaska Corporation, the regional Native corporation established under the Alaska Native Claims Settlement Act.

4. The U.S. Forest Service, University of Alaska, Fairbanks, for example, undertook a three-phase vulnerability assessment of potential impacts related to climate change. The study indicates that the park is high risk and advises creating plans to address the uncertainty. See https://accap.uaf.edu/project/tongass-national-forest-climate-change-vulnerability-assessment, accessed July 12, 2016.

5. It is not my claim that team members were unaware; I talked in depth with two members who shared their thoughts on the ongoing and seemingly intractable conflicts related to forest management. I also spoke at length with a respected Tlingit elder who shared her thoughts on the region's history and cultural issues.

6. I make a distinction between cultural landscapes and heritage landscapes. Whereas both share similar "inventories," the term *heritage landscapes* places the attention on the historical and sociopolitical contexts of landscapes *as* heritage. Locating these contexts of heritage landscapes within contemporary debates and discussions is essential. Frequently, they are enmeshed in and central to land rights and native title claims, bioprospecting contracts, biotechnology patents, water rights, ecosystem inventories, and cultural and natural heritage nominations to the World Heritage list. Yet, they are often not identified as such.

7. Morrison (1993:432, quoted in Gill 1997:170) used the term "human spill" to talk about the influx of industry representatives, cleanup crews, academics, and other groups that were part of the cleanup and recovery efforts.

8. Johnson and Rustin (2013:xx–xxi) reviewed more than twenty thousand documents and provide a concise overview of important scientific studies, resources such as websites and libraries, and reference to scientific meetings and conferences.

9. For more on the Trustee Council, including publications, policies, procedures, and the status of restoration projects, see http://www.evostc.state.ak.us/index.cfm?FA=aboutUs.home, accessed January 30, 2015.

10. Congress established the Prince William Sound Oil Spill Recovery Institute (OSRI) to document effects on the natural resources, environments, and economic well-being of the communities in the Sound and to develop best practices for dealing with oil spills. For more on OSRI see http://www.pws-osri.org, accessed January 30, 2015.

11. To undertake archaeological work within the spill area and to record damages to cultural resources, the *Exxon Valdez* Cultural Resource Program obtained nine Archaeological Resources Protection Act and Special Use permits from the Alaska Office of History and Archaeology, National Park Service, U.S. Fish and Wildlife Service, and U.S. Forest Service (see Mobley 1990).

12. Alaska Native groups in the Chugach region, for example, reported startling consequences to the subsistence levels that range from 46 percent to nearly 60 percent after the spill. Similarly, hunters now have to spend more time and travel farther to hunt for sea mammals. See https://www.chugachmiut.org/history.html, last accessed March 11, 2015.

13. For a discussion on climate change and impacts see, e.g., Fernández-Giménez et al. 2012; Rudaya et al. 2009.

14. More can be found at http://www.spiegel.de/international/archeological-sensation-ancient-mummy-found-in-mongolia-a-433600.html, accessed May 21, 2015.

15. *Discover Magazine* published a short article on the work by German archaeologist Hermann Parzinger, who worked with a team of archaeologists and Russian geophysicists to locate potential tombs in the permafrost. Our research team visited their extensive camp, which included nearly thirty researchers (and their flags!) from Mongolia, Russia, and Germany. For more on the 2006 find, see http://discovermagazine.com/2008/jul/25-frozen-siberian-mummies-reveal-a-lost-civilization, last accessed July 15, 2016.

16. Biosphere reserves are recognized within the UNESCO Man and the Biosphere Programme to encourage signatories to the World Heritage Convention to promote biodiversity conservation and sustainable development. The Altai region is also a UNESCO World Heritage site, first inscribed on the UNESCO World Heritage List in 1998, for the Golden Mounts of Altai, and again in 2011 with the Petroglyphic Complexes of the Mongolian Altai.

Chapter 4. Experts and Epistemologies

1. For discussions on cultural heritage experts see John Schofield's (2014) edited volume, especially his introduction to the book, and articles by Denis Byrne (1991) and Dominic Boyer (2008). But see Meskell (2016:75) for a cautionary note.

2. The project involved questionnaires, in-depth semi-structured interviews, ethnographic observation, and discourse analyses of reports, archives, and professional activities. I observed and recorded experts in a broad range of settings, from in the field to conferences and as "experts"; I also conducted interviews with professional experts on their ideal strategies, the composition of their community, and their views on the profession.

3. See http://www.worldbank.org/en/news/loans-credits/2012/04/12/lebanon-cultural-heritage-urban-development-project, accessed May 1, 2015.

4. A master's thesis by Mark Guarnaccia (2015), then a student at City University of New

York, provides an extensive overview of this project, and particularly a critique of the heritage as development model.

5. Of note, that same year (1992) the World Heritage Committee created the cultural land-scape designation as a way to address divisions between cultural and natural heritage.

6. As the IWGIA noted, "Culture, as the underpinning foundation of Sustainable Develop-ment, has not been recognized, despite some reference to the importance of culture in sustain-able development." See http://www.iwgia.org/news/search-news?news_id=533, accessed May 27, 2015.

7. The Millennium Ecosystem Assessment is a United Nations initiative to assess "the con-sequences of ecosystem change for human well-being and the scientific basis for action needed to enhance the conservation and sustainable use of those systems and their contribution to human well-being." The initiative involved nearly fourteen hundred experts and resulted in a report outlining the condition of world's ecosystems. See http://www.millenniumassessment. org/en/About.html, accessed May 15, 2015.

8. For example, in 2011 Dow Chemical Company collaborated with the Nature Conser-vancy to implement an ecosystem services framework into all of its business planning and operations (Ingram et al. 2012). See http://www.dow.com/en-us/science-and-sustainability/collaborations/nature-conservancy, accessed May 26, 2015.

9. For more on the sometimes contentious debates over the role of culture and conserva-tion, see Agrawal and Redford 2009; Curran et al. 2009; Inglis and Bone 2006; Kopnina 2012; Redford and Sanderson 2000; and Terborgh 2000. It is interesting to note that communities are often framed as either key drivers in environmental impacts (Oates 1999) or as central to conservation approaches (Hughes 2006).

10. See http://www.iucn.org/about/work/programmes/gpap_home/pas_gpap, accessed May 1, 2015.

11. See https://www.iucn.org/about/work/programmes/economics/econ_ourwork/econ_currentprojects, accessed May 15, 2015.

12. See http://whc.unesco.org/en/list/722, accessed May 5, 2015.

Chapter 5. Landscapes of Extraction

1. This statement is based on reports from a variety of state and federal agencies, including the Departments of Mines and Petroleum, Mining Council Australia, Australian Bureau of Statistics, Chamber of Minerals and Energy of Western Australia, Department of Regional Development and Lands, Real Estate Institute of Western Australia, and Western Australian Council of Social Service.

While in the field, I drew upon my experience as an ethnographer and anthropologist (and archaeologist) working in Indigenous cultural landscapes (survey, record, and document). I interviewed industry representatives, Aboriginal members, and international heritage scholars involved in research or industry in the Pilbara and in Western Australia and the Northern Territory more broadly. From this research I selected two case studies: the Burrup Peninsula and Onslow. I chose the Burrup Peninsula because of the local Indigenous community's strong connections with the site, involvement in heritage negotiations, and ties to industry. In con-trast, Onslow has had less participation from local stakeholders. I wanted to investigate if and how industry has used cultural and environmental heritage to promote its projects. My project also investigates institutions (mining and heritage experts) and builds on my institutional ethnography of heritage experts and conservation managers in World Heritage contexts.

2. For discussions on resource industries in Western Australia see Altman 2003; Altman and Martin 2009; Scambary 2013.

3. *Country* is the term Aboriginal people use to describe their ancestral and inherited places and the practices that guide their behavior. Aboriginal elders hold and pass down the knowledge of the Law and how it should be used; the Law is all-encompassing and guides people's relationships to land, to others, and to all forms of life. Knowledge of Country is central to the well-being and cultural survival of Indigenous Australians. As such, Aboriginal people have an obligation to care for Country, including visiting sites and maintaining knowledge of the land and animals that may not always be recognized by outsiders (B. Rose 1995:12).

4. A significant literature exists that examines mining and Indigenous peoples in Australia (see e.g., Cousins and Nieuwenhuysen 1984; Howitt et al. 1996; Weiner and Glaskin 2007). Outside Australia, Ballard and Banks (2003) provide an excellent overview.

5. We are seeing more partnerships with Traditional Owners beyond the Australian context. In 2010, for example, the Haisla Nation of British Columbia entered into a thirty-year agreement with Rio Tinto Alcan to support aluminum operations and with the government to fast-track an LNG plant. Yet, while the company works with Traditional Owners, other stakeholders and environmental groups have protested the lack of environmental oversight.

6. See http://www.stockhouse.com/news/financialnewsdetailfeeds.aspx?n=14847180&src =cp, last accessed May 1, 2014.

7. It is beyond the scope of the discussion here, but an interesting debate concerning Rio Tinto Limited and the World Archaeological Congress was published by Nick Shepherd and Alejandro Haber (2011). See also the responses by Domingo-Sanz (2012) and C. Smith (2011).

8. The Brundlandt Report, *Our Common Future,* provided a definition of sustainability that has been enormously influential in mining contexts. It defined sustainability as "development that meets the needs of the present without compromising the ability of future generations to meet their own needs" (World Commission on Environment and Development 1987). As Scambary (2013:12) pointed out, this definition of sustainable development has had broad appeal to the mining industry. The crux is in how industry has applied and misapplied the definition.

9. A mining boom has been defined as a "significant increase in mining investment or mining output" (Battelino 2010:63).

10. A significant analysis and discussion on this subject was presented by Benedict Scambary (2013), who analyzed agreements made between Aboriginal Australians and the mining industry.

11. Aboriginal scholar Marcia Langton (2012, 2013) argues that participation in the mining economy is the way toward poverty reduction and transforming Indigenous communities (see also Langton and Longbottom 2012).

12. Davidson et al. (2014) provide a broad overview of the Burrup. See also McDonald and Veth 2009; Veth 2015.

13. As of June 9, 2015, the bill had reached the Second Reading in the Lower House, and was restored to the Legislative Assembly notice paper in February 2015. The current status of the bill can be found at http://www.parliament.wa.gov.au/parliament/Bills.nsf/BillProgressPopup ?openForm&ParentUNID=E863020A2E318B6A48257D9D000BC478, accessed June 9, 2015.

14. The DAA's minister for aboriginal affairs, Peter Collier, released a media statement on November 27, 2014. For more on this see http://www.daa.wa.gov.au/en/Heritage-and-Culture/Aboriginal-Heritage-Legislative-Changes, accessed June 9, 2015.

15. Australian ABC news reporter Katrin Long interviewed and reported on a protest of over sixty Traditional Owners and elders who petitioned outside Parliament, including more than sixteen hundred signatures. Long included quotes from Collier that can be found at http://www.abc.net.au/news/2014-11-20/protest-against-changes-to-aboriginal-heritage-act/5906040, accessed June 12, 2015.

16. Marina Welker (2009:145–146) provides a comprehensive overview of CSR, including its important features and the rise of CSR in the 1990s (see also Luning 2012; Rajak 2011; Shamir 2010).

17. See http://www.diamondroute.com/sustainability.htm, accessed June 15, 2015.

18. See http://savethewildup.org/2014/04/swup-president-to-mdeq-regulate-dont-faciliate, accessed May 1, 2014.

19. See http://www.washingtonpost.com/national/health-science/agencies-urge-interior-to-reject-mining-near-national-park/2012/02/03/gIQA8YtBoQ_story.html, last accessed April 20, 2014.

Chapter 6. Toward a Critical Theory of Heritage

1. Earlier engagements were often tense, as in the example of Conzinc Rio Tinto and the Marandoo mine, where archaeologists (and others) worked on behalf of the Traditional Owners to protect rights. The Western Australia Parliament responded with the passing of the 1992 Aboriginal Heritage (Marandoo) Act, which in effect removed these lands from heritage protection. The Traditional Owners organized and appealed, and a positive outcome was that Rio Tinto took seriously the issues that were coming to the fore and created agreements with claimants (Veth 2015). Today the Marandoo mine is part of Karijini National Park, that is presently "co-managed" by Traditional Owners and the Department of Parks and Wildlife.

2. Hamersley Iron originally established the mine within the park boundaries, but the mine was later removed from the park boundaries due to intense protests from Indigenous groups, as well as the general public, over the destruction of sacred sites.

3. The "After Oil" project is a collaborative partnership that seeks to address impacts of oil and how these intersect with built environments, social dynamics, educational systems, and cultures. See http://afteroil.ca, accessed August 12, 2016.

References Cited

Agrawal, Arun, and Kent H. Redford
2009   Conservation and Displacement: An Overview. *Conservation and Society* 7(1):1–10.
Akiwumi, Fenda A.
2014   Strangers and Sierra Leone Mining: Cultural Heritage and Sustainable Development Challenges. *Journal of Cleaner Production* 84:773–782.
Albrecht, Glenn, and Neville Ellis
2014   The Ethics of Resource Extraction and Processing: Two Western Australian Case Studies. In *Resource Curse or Cure? On the Sustainability of Development in Western Australia*, edited by Martin Brueckner, Angela Durey, Robyn Mayes, and Christof Pforr, pp. 43–57. Springer, London.
Al-Hagla, S. Khalid
2010   Sustainable Urban Development in Historical Areas Using the Tourist Trail Approach: A Case Study of the Cultural Heritage and Urban Development (CHUD) Project in Saida, Lebanon. *Cities* 27(4):234–248.
Altman, Jon C.
2003   People on Country, Healthy Landscapes and Sustainable Indigenous Economic Futures: The Arnhem Land Case. *The Drawing Board: An Australian Review of Public Affairs* 4(2):65–82.
Altman, Jon C., and David Martin
2009   *Power, Culture, Economy: Indigenous Australians and Mining*. Australian National University E Press, Canberra.
American Association of Museums
2002   *Mastering Civic Engagement: A Challenge to Museums*. American Association of Museums, Washington, D.C.
Anker, Kristen
2007   The Unofficial Law of Native Title: Indigenous Rights, State Recognition and Legal Pluralism in Australia. Unpublished Ph.D. dissertation, Department of Law, University of Sydney.
Anschuetz, Kurt F., Richard H. Wilshusen, and Cherie L. Scheick
2001   An Archaeology of Landscapes: Perspectives and Directions. *Journal of Archaeological Research* 9(2):157–211.
Armitage, Andrew
1995   *Comparing the Policy of Aboriginal Assimilation: Australia, Canada, and New Zealand*. University of British Columbia Press, Vancouver.

Arnold, Caroline, and Arthur Arnold

2003   *Uluru: Australia's Aboriginal Heart.* Houghton Mifflin Harcourt, New York.

Ashmore, Wendy, and A. Bernard Knapp (editors)

1999   *Archaeologies of Landscape: Contemporary Perspectives.* Blackwell, Malden, Mass.

Atalay, Sonya

2012   *Community-Based Archaeology: Research with, by and for Indigenous and Local Communities.* University of California Press, Berkeley.

Badenkov, Yuri

2011   Transboundary Issues in the Altai. *Mountain Research and Development* 31(4):390–391.

Baird, Melissa F.

2003   Analysis of the Clam Cove (49-SEL-006) and Tuxedni Bay (49-SEL-229) Pictograph Sites, Lake Clark National Park and Preserve, Alaska. Unpublished Master's thesis, Department of Anthropology, University of Oregon, Eugene.

2006a   Frederica de Laguna and the Study of Pre-Contact Pictographs from Coastal Sites in Cook Inlet and Prince William Sound, Alaska. *Arctic Anthropology* 43(2):136–147.

2006b   The Prince William Sound Rock Art Recording Project, Summer 2005. Final report submitted to the Chugach National Forest, Alaska Region and the Chugach Alaska Corporation. On file. Chugach National Forest, Anchorage, Alaska.

2009   The Politics of Place: Heritage, Identity, and the Epistemologies of Cultural Landscapes, Unpublished dissertation, Department of Anthropology, University of Oregon, Eugene.

2013   "The Breath of the Mountain Is My Heart": Indigenous Cultural Landscapes and the Politics of Heritage. *International Journal of Heritage Studies* 19(4):327–340.

2014   Heritage, Human Rights, and Social Justice. *Heritage & Society* 7(2):139–155.

2015   Heritage Ecologies and the Rhetoric of Nature. In *Heritage Keywords: Rhetoric and Redescription in Cultural Heritage*, edited by K. Lafrenz Samuels and T. Rico, pp. 207–220. University of Colorado Press, Boulder.

Baird, Melissa F., and Ruthann Knudson

2012   In the Spirit of Old Friends: Reflections on Repatriation at Agate Fossil Beds National Monument, Nebraska. *Heritage of the Great Plains* 41(2):34–48.

Ballard, Chris, and Glenn Banks

2003   Resource Wars: The Anthropology of Mining. *Annual Review of Anthropology* 32:287–313.

Balter, Michael

2015   Big Archaeology Fights Big Oil to Preserve Ancient Landscape. *Science* 349(6250):774–775.

Barney, Keith

2009   Laos and the Making of a Relational Resource Frontier. *Geographical Journal* 175(2):146–159.

Basso, Keith H.

1996   *Wisdom Sits in Places: Landscapes and Language among the Western Apache.* University of New Mexico Press, Albuquerque.

Battellino, Ric

2010   Mining Booms and the Australian Economy: Address to the Sydney Institute. *Reserve Bank Bulletin* March:63–69.

Battiste, Marie A., and James Y. Henderson
2000   *Protecting Indigenous Knowledge and Heritage.* Purich, Saskatoon, SK.

Bednarik, Robert G.
2011   The Dampier Campaign. *Rock Art Research* 28(1):1.

Beier, Colin M., Amy Lauren Lovecraft, and F. Stuart Chapin
2009   Growth and Collapse of a Resource System: An Adaptive Cycle of Change in Public Lands Governance and Forest Management in Alaska. *Ecology and Society* 14(2), https://www.treesearch.fs.fed.us/pubs/37719, accessed May 28, 2017.

Benjamin, Walter
2003   *Selected Writings, Volume 4.* Belknap Press, Cambridge, Mass.

Bennetts, Stephen
2015   WA's New-Look Aboriginal Heritage Policy and the Assessment of Sacred Sites: When Is an Aboriginal Sacred Site Not a Sacred Site? *The Monthly*, 17 February. https://www.themonthly.com.au/blog/stephen-bennetts/2015/17/2015/1424128413/wa-s-new-look-aboriginal-heritage-policy-and, accessed June 15, 2015.

Berkes, Fikret
1999   *Sacred Ecology: Traditional Ecological Knowledge and Resource Management.* Taylor and Francis, Ann Arbor, Mich.

Blue Spruce, Duane, and Tanya Thrasher
2008   *The Land Has Memory: Indigenous Knowledge, Native Landscapes, and the National Museum of the American Indian.* University of North Carolina Press, Chapel Hill.

Boer, Ben, and Graeme Wiffen
2006   *Heritage Law in Australia.* Oxford University Press, South Melbourne.

Bolin, Annalisa
2012   On the Side of Light: Performing Morality at Rwanda's Genocide Memorials. *Journal of Conflict Archaeology* 7(3):199–207.

Borch, Merete
2001   Rethinking the Origins of *Terra Nullius. Australian Historical Studies* (117):222–239.

Bourdieu, Pierre
1977   *Outline of a Theory of Practice.* Cambridge University Press, Cambridge.

Bourgeois, Jean, Alain De Wulf, Rudi Goossens, and Wouter Gheyle
2007   Saving the Frozen Scythian Tombs of the Altai Mountains (Central Asia). *World Archaeology* 39(3):458–474.

Bowdler, Sandra
1988   Repainting Australian Rock Art. *Antiquity* 62(236):517–523.

Boyer, Dominic
2005   The Corporeality of Expertise. *Ethnos* 70(2):243–266.
2008   Thinking Through the Anthropology of Experts. *Anthropology in Action* 15(2): 38–46.

Bradshaw, Elizabeth, and Rio Tinto
2011   *Why Cultural Heritage Matters: A Resource Guide for Integrating Cultural Heritage Management into Communities Work at Rio Tinto.* Rio Tinto, London.

Braun, Bruce
2002   *The Intemperate Rainforest: Nature, Culture, and Power on Canada's West Coast.* University of Minnesota Press, Minneapolis.

Breglia, Lisa

2006   *Monumental Ambivalence: The Politics of Heritage.* University of Texas Press, Austin.

2013   *Living with Oil: Promises, Peaks, and Declines on Mexico's Gulf Coast.* University of Texas Press, Austin.

Brueckner, Martin, Angela Durey, Robyn Mayes, and Christof Pforr

2014   Confronting the "Resource Curse of Cure" Binary. In *Resource Curse or Cure? On the Sustainability of Development in Western Australia*, edited by M. Brueckner, A. Durey, R. Mayes and C. Pforr, pp. 3–23. Springer, London.

Byrne, Denis

1991   Western Hegemony in Archaeological Heritage Management. *History and Anthropology* 5(2):269–276.

1996   Deep Nation: Australia's Acquisition of an Indigenous Past. *Aboriginal History* 20:82–107.

2003a   Nervous Landscapes: Race and Space in Australia. *Journal of Social Archaeology* 3(2):169–193.

2003b   The Ethos of Return: Erasure and Reinstatement of Aboriginal Visibility in the Australian Historical Landscape. *Historical Archaeology* 37(1):73–86.

Calma, Graeme, and Lynette Liddle

2002   *Uluṟu-Kata Tjuṯa National Park: Sustainable Management and Development.* World Heritage Papers 7, Manuscript on file at the ICOMOS Documentation Centre, Paris.

Carman, John

2000   Theorising a Realm of Practice? Introducing Archaeological Heritage Management as a Research Field. *International Journal of Heritage Studies* 6(4):303–308.

2005   *Against Cultural Property: Archaeology, Heritage and Ownership.* Duckworth, London.

Carr, E. Summerson

2010   Enactments of Expertise. *Annual Review of Anthropology* 39:17–32.

Carruthers, Jane

2003   Contesting Cultural Landscapes in South Africa and Australia: Comparing the Significance of the Kalahari Gemsbok and Uluṟu-Kata Tjuṯa National Parks. In *Disputed Territories: Land, Culture and Identity in Settler Societies*, edited by D. Trigger and G. Griffiths, pp. 233–268. Hong Kong University Press, Hong Kong.

Carter, Paul

1987   *The Road to Botany Bay: An Exploration of Landscape and History.* University of Chicago Press, Chicago.

Casella, Eleanor C.

2007   *The Archaeology of Institutional Confinement.* University Press of Florida, Gainesville.

Casey, Edward S.

1996   How to Get from Space to Place in a Fairly Short Stretch of Time: Phenomenological Prolegomena. In *Senses of Place*, edited by Steven Feld and Keith H. Basso, pp. 3–12. School of American Research Press, Sante Fe.

Central Land Council

2003   *Uluṟu-Kata Tjuṯa National Park.* http://www.clc.org.au/publications/content/looking-after-country-the-clc-ranger, accessed May 25,2017.

Cernea, Michael M.

2001   *Cultural Heritage and Development: A Framework for Action in the Middle East and North Africa.* The World Bank, Washington, D.C.

Cernea, Michael M., and Kai Schmidt-Soltau

2006   Poverty Risks and National Parks: Policy Issues in Conservation and Resettlement. *World Development* 34(10):1808–1830.

Chakrabarty, Dipesh

2008   The Public Life of History: An Argument out of India. *Public Culture* 20:143–168.

Chan, Kai Ming Adam, Lara Hoshizaki, and Brian Klinkenberg

2011   Ecosystem Services in Conservation Planning: Targeted Benefits vs. Co-Benefits or Costs? *PLoS One* 6(9):e24378.

Chan, Kai M. A., Terre Satterfield, and Joshua Goldstein

2012   Rethinking Ecosystem Services to Better Address and Navigate Cultural Values. *Ecological Economics* 74:8–18.

Chesterman, John, and Brian Galligan

1997   *Citizens without Rights: Aborigines and Australian Citizenship.* Cambridge University Press, Cambridge.

Chiesura, Anna, and Rudolf de Groot

2003   Critical Natural Capital: A Socio-Cultural Perspective. *Ecological Economics* (44): 219–231.

Cleere, Henry

2001   The Uneasy Bedfellows: Universality and Cultural Heritage. In *Destruction and Conservation of Cultural Property*, edited by R. Layton, J. Thomas, and P. G. Stone, pp. 22–29. Routledge, London.

Colwell-Chanthaphonh, Chip, and Thomas J. Ferguson

2006   Memory Pieces and Footprints: Multivocality and the Meanings of Ancient Times and Ancestral Places among the Zuni and Hopi. *American Anthropologist* 108(1): 148–162.

Colwell-Chanthaphonh, Chip, and Thomas John Ferguson (editors)

2007   *Collaboration in Archaeological Practice: Engaging Descendant Communities.* AltaMira, Rowman, Md.

Comaroff, John L., and Jean Comaroff

2009   *Ethnicity, Inc.* University of Chicago Press, Chicago.

Conniff, Richard

2012   What's Wrong with Putting a Price on Nature? *Guardian Environment Network* 18 October:1–8.

Connor, Michael

2005   *The Invention of Terra Nullius: Historical and Legal Fictions on the Foundation of Australia.* Macleay Press, Paddington, NSW.

Conradin, Katharina, and Thomas Hammer

2016   Making the Most of World Natural Heritage: Linking Conservation and Sustainable Regional Development? *Sustainability* 8(4):323.

Coombe, Rosemary J., and Melissa F. Baird

2015   The Limits of Heritage: Corporate Interests and Cultural Rights on Resource Frontiers. In *A Companion to Heritage Studies*, edited by William Logan, Máiréad Nic Craith, and Ullrich Kockel, pp. 337–354. Wiley Blackwell, Malden, Mass.

Coombe, Rosemary J., and Lindsay M. Weiss

2015   Neoliberalism, Heritage Regimes, and Cultural Rights. In *Global Heritage: A Reader*, edited by L. Meskell, pp. 43–69. Wiley Blackwell, Malden, Mass.

Coombes, Annie E.

2003   *History after Apartheid: Visual Culture and Public Memory in a Democratic South Africa*. Duke University Press, Durham, N.C.

Cousins, David, and John Nieuwenhuysen

1984   *Aboriginals and the Mining Industry: Case Studies of the Australian Experience*. Allen & Unwin, Crows Nest, New South Wales.

Cowan, Jane K.

2006   Culture and Rights after Culture and Rights. *American Anthropologist* 108(1):9–24.

Cowan, Jane K., and Richard A. Wilson

2001   *Culture and Rights: Anthropological Perspectives*. Cambridge University Press, Cambridge.

Crowell, Aron L., and Daniel H. Mann

1998   *Archeology and Coastal Dynamics of Kenai Fjords National Park, Alaska*. National Park Service Alaska Region, Research/Resources Management Report AR/RCR-98-34.

Cruikshank, Julie

2005   *Do Glaciers Listen? Local Knowledge, Colonial Encounters, and Social Imagination*. University of British Columbia Press, Vancouver.

Curran, Bryan, Terry Sunderland, Fiona Maisels, John Oates, Stella Asaha, Michael Balinga, Louis Defo, Andrew Dunn, Paul Telfer, Leonard Usongo, Karin von Loebenstein, and Philipp Roth

2009   Are Central Africa's Protected Areas Displacing Hundreds of Thousands of Rural Poor? *Conservation and Society* 7(1):30–45.

Daily, Gretchen, and Katherine Ellison

2002   *The New Economy of Nature: The Quest to Make Conservation Profitable*. Island Press, Washington, D.C.

Davidson, Iain, Tim Douglas, and Wilfred Hicks

2014   Burrup Peninsula. In *Encyclopedia of Global Archaeology*, edited by C. Smith, pp. 1082–1086. Springer Press, New York.

Davidson, Robyn

2011   Into the Beehive: The Destruction of Burrup Rock Art. *The Monthly*. February: 22–29.

Dawson, Peter

2015   On Self-Determination and Constitutional Recognition. *Indigenous Law Bulletin* 8(16):3–6.

De Beers

2014   De Beers Funds New Project to Address the Impact of Roads on Our Wildlife. Press release, 17 October. https://www.ewt.org.za/media/2014/DE%20BEERS%20 FUNDS%20NEW%20PROJECT%20TO%20ADDRESS%20THE%20IMPACT%20 OF%20ROADS%20ON%20OUR%20WILDLIFE.pdf, accessed May 16, 2017.

de la Cadena, Marisol

2010   Indigenous Cosmopolitics in the Andes: Conceptual Reflections beyond Politics. *Cultural Anthropology* 25(2):334–370.

De Lacy, Terry

1994   The Uluṟu/Kakadu Model–Aṉangu *Tjukurpa*: 50,000 Years of Aboriginal Law and Land Management Changing the Concept of National Parks in Australia. *Society and Natural Resources* (7):479–498.

De Lacy, Terry, and Bruce Lawson

1997   The Uluṟu-Kakadu Model: Joint Management of Aboriginal Owned National Parks in Australia. In *Conservation through Cultural Survival: Indigenous Peoples and Protected Areas*, edited by Stan Stevens, pp. 155–188. Island Press, Washington, D.C.

de Laguna, Frederica

1934   *The Archaeology of Cook Inlet, Alaska*. University of Pennsylvania Press, Philadelphia.

1956   *Chugach Prehistory: The Archaeology of Prince William Sound, Alaska*. University of Washington Press, Seattle.

Dobrin, Sidney I., and Christian R. Weisser

2002   *Natural Discourse: Toward Ecocomposition*. SUNY Press, Albany.

Dombrowski, Kirk

2002   The Praxis of Indigenism and Alaska Native Timber Politics. *American Anthropologist* 104:1062–1073.

Domingo-Sanz, Inés

2012   WAC Matters: A Different View to That of Shepherd and Haber. *Archaeologies* 8(1): 2–11.

Du Cros, Hillary, and C. Johnston

2002   Tourism Tracks and Sacred Places: Pashupatinath and Uluṟu: Case Studies from Nepal and Australia. *Historic Environment* (16):38–42.

Dubuisson, Eva-Marie, and Anna Genina

2011   Claiming an Ancestral Homeland: Kazakh Pilgrimage and Migration in Inner Asia. *Central Asian Survey* 30(3–4):469–485.

Durbin, Kathie

2005   *Tongass: Pulp Politics and the Fight for the Alaskan Rainforest*. Oregon State University Press, Corvallis.

Echo-Hawk, Roger C.

2000   Ancient History in the New World: Integrating Oral Traditions and the Archaeological Record in Deep Time. *American Antiquity* 65(2):267–290.

Economist

2014   The New Silk Road: Stretching the Threads. *The Economist*. 27 November. http://www.economist.com/news/china/21635061-impoverished-south-west-china-seeks-become-economic-hub-stretching-threads, accessed June 15, 2015.

Edmunds, Mary

2013   *A Good Life: Human Rights and Encounters with Modernity*. Australian National University E Press, Canberra.

Ekern, Stener, William Logan, Birgitte Sauge, and Amund Sinding-Larsen

2012   Human Rights and World Heritage: Preserving Our Common Dignity through

Rights-Based Approaches to Site Management. *International Journal of Heritage Studies* 18(3):213–225.

Everard, Mark, Rory Harrington, and Robert J. McInnes

2012   Facilitating Implementation of Landscape-Scale Water Management: The Integrated Constructed Wetland Concept. *Ecosystem Services* 2:27–37.

Evers, Sandra, Gwyn Campbell, and Michael Lambek

2013   *Contest for Land in Madagascar: Environment, Ancestors and Development.* African Social Studies Series. Brill, Leiden.

Fairhead, James, and Melissa Leach

1996   *Misreading the African Landscape: Society and Ecology in a Forest-Savannah Mosaic.* Cambridge University Press, Cambridge.

Fanon, Frantz

1968   *The Wretched of the Earth.* Grove Press, New York.

Feld, Steven, and Keith Basso

1996   Introduction. In *Senses of Place*, edited by Steven Feld and Keith H. Basso, pp. 3–12. School of American Research Press, Sante Fe.

Fernández-Giménez, M., B. Batjav, and B. Baival

2012   *Lessons from the Dzud: Adaptation and Resilience in Mongolian Pastoral Socio-Ecological Systems.* World Bank, Washington, D.C.

Findley, Lisa

2005   *Building Change: Architecture, Politics and Cultural Agency.* Routledge, London.

Flanagan, Frances

nd   The Burrup Agreement: A Case Study in Future Act Negotiation. *Agreements, Treaties and Negotiated Settlements Project.* http://www.atns.net.au/atns/references/attachments/Flanagan%20Paper.pdf, accessed May 25, 2017.

Fletcher, Christine

1999   Living Together but Not as Neighbours: Cultural Imperialism in Australia. In *Indigenous Peoples' Rights in Australia, Canada, and New Zealand*, edited by Paul Havemann, pp. 335–350. Oxford University Press, Auckland.

Flood, Josephine

2006   *The Original Australians: The Story of the Aboriginal People.* Allen & Unwin, Crows Nest, NSW.

Fontein, Joost

2006   *The Silence of Great Zimbabwe: Contested Landscapes and the Power of Heritage.* University College London Press, London.

Fowler, Peter

2004   *Landscapes for the World: Conserving a Global Heritage.* Windgather Press, Macclesfield, UK.

Ganapathy, Sandhya

2013   Imagining Alaska: Local and Translocal Engagements with Place. *American Anthropologist* 115(1):96–111.

Giddens, Anthony

1984   *The Constitution of Society: Outline of the Theory of Structuration.* University of California Press, Berkeley.

Gilbert, Jérémie

2010   Custodians of the Land: Indigenous Peoples, Human Rights and Cultural Integrity. In *Cultural Diversity, Heritage and Human Rights: Intersections in Theory and Practice*, edited by Michele Langfield, William Logan, and Máiréad Nic Craith, pp. 31–44. Routledge, London.

Gill, Duane A.

1997   The Day the Water Died: Cultural Impacts of the *Exxon Valdez* Oil Spill on Alaska Natives. In *The "Exxon Valdez" Disaster: Readings on a Modern Social Problem*, edited by J. S. Picou, D. A. Gill and M. J. Cohen, pp. 167–191. Kendall/Hunt, Dubuque, Iowa.

Gnecco, Cristóbal, and Patricia Ayala

2011   *Indigenous Peoples and Archaeology in Latin America*. Left Coast Press, Walnut Creek, Calif.

Godden, Lee, Marcia Langton, Odette Mazel, and Maureen Tehan

2008   Introduction: Accommodating Interests in Resource Extraction: Indigenous Peoples, Local Communities and the Role of Law in Economic and Social Sustainability. *Journal of Energy & Natural Resources Law* 26(1):1–30.

Goggin, Peter N.

2013   *Environmental Rhetoric and Ecologies of Place*. Routledge, London.

Goldman, Michael

2005   *Imperial Nature: The World Bank and Struggles for Social Justice in the Age of Globalization*. Yale University Press, New Haven.

Golub, Alex

2014   *Leviathans at the Gold Mine: Creating Indigenous and Corporate Actors in Papua New Guinea*. Duke University Press, Durham, N.C.

Golub, Alex, and Mooweon Rhee

2013   Traction: The Role of Executives in Localising Global Mining and Petroleum Industries in Papua New Guinea. *Paideuma* 59:215–236.

Gonzalez, Rhodera

2000   Platforms and Terraces: Bridging Participation and GIS in Joint-Learning for Watershed Management with the Ifugao of the Philippines. Unpublished Ph.D. dissertation, Wagenigen University, Netherlands.

González-Ruibal, Alfredo

2008   A Time to Destroy: An Archaeology of Supermodernity. *Current Anthropology* 49(2): 247–279.

Gordillo, Gastón

2014   *Rubble: The Afterlife of Destruction*. Duke University Press, Durham, N.C.

Gordon, Michael

2011   Landmark Rio Deal to Deliver Billions to Aborigines. *The Age,* 3 June. http://www.theage.com.au/national/landmark-rio-deal-to-deliver-billionsto-aborigines-20110602-1fiwq.html, accessed November 1, 2014.

Greene, Shane

2004   Indigenous People Incorporated? Culture as Politics, Culture as Property in Pharmaceutical Bioprospecting. *Current Anthropology* 45(2):211–237.

Greenough, Paul, and Anna Lowenhaupt Tsing (editors)
2003   *Nature in the Global South: Environmental Projects in South and Southeast Asia.* Duke University Press, Durham, N.C.

Griffin, Graham
2002   Welcome to Aboriginal Land: Anangu Ownership and Management of Uluru–Kata Tjuta National Park. In *Conservation and Mobile Indigenous Peoples: Displacement, Forced Settlement, and Sustainable Development,* edited by Dawn Chatty and Marcus Colchester, pp. 362–376. Berghahn, New York.

Guarnaccia, Mark
2015   The World Bank, Amartya Sen and Cultural Heritage as Development in Jordan. *CUNY Academic Works.* http://academicworks.cuny.edu/gc_etds/956, accessed May 25, 2017.

Guimbatan, Rachel, and Teddy Baguilat
2006   Misunderstanding the Notion of Conservation in the Philippine Rice Terraces Cultural Landscapes. *International Social Science Journal* 58(187):59–67.

Hafsaas-Tsakos, Henriette
2011   Ethical Implications of Salvage Archaeology and Dam Building: The Clash between Archaeologists and Local People in Dar al-Manasir, Sudan. *Journal of Social Archaeology* 11(1):49–76.

Hanable, William S., and Carol Burkhart
1990   The *Exxon Valdez* Oil Spill and the National Park Service: A Report on the Initial Response. On file. National Park Service, Alaska Region, Anchorage.

Haraway, Donna J.
2016   *Staying with the Trouble: Making Kin in the Chthulucene.* Duke University Press, Durham, N.C.

Harney, W. E. (Bill)
1963   *To Ayers Rock and Beyond.* Robert Hale, London.

Harrison, Otto R.
1991   An Overview of the *Exxon Valdez* Oil Spill. *Proceedings, International Oil Spill Conference* 1991:313–319.

Harrison, Rodney
2010   *Understanding the Politics of Heritage.* Manchester University Press, Manchester.
2011   Surface Assemblages: Toward an Archaeology in and of the Present. *Archaeological Dialogues* 18(2):141–161.
2013   *Heritage: Critical Approaches.* Routledge, London.

Harvey, David C.
2001   Heritage Pasts and Heritage Presents: Temporality, Meaning, and the Scope of Heritage Studies. *International Journal of Heritage Studies* 7(4):319–338.

Haslam Mckenzie, Fiona
2013   Delivering Enduring Benefits from a Gas Development: Governance and Planning Challenges in Remote Western Australia. *Australian Geographer* 44(3):341–358.

Havemann, Paul (editor)
1999   *Indigenous Peoples' Rights in Australia, Canada, and New Zealand.* Oxford University Press, Auckland.

Hayden, Cori

2003 *When Nature Goes Public: The Making and Unmaking of Bioprospecting in Mexico.* Princeton University Press, Princeton, N.J.

Heidegger, Martin

1977 *Basic Writings.* Harper and Row, New York.

Helmreich, Stefan

2009 *Alien Ocean: Anthropological Voyages in Microbial Seas.* University of California Press, Berkeley.

Henare, Amiria

2007 Taonga Maori: Encompassing Rights and Property in New Zealand. In *Thinking through Things: Theorising Artefacts Ethnographically,* edited by A. Henare, M. Holbraad and S. Wastell, pp. 47–67. Routledge, London.

Henry, Doug

2005 Anthropological Contributions to the Study of Disasters. In *Disciplines, Disasters and Emergency Management: The Convergence of Concepts Issues and Trends from the Research Literature,* edited by D. McEntire and W. B. Blanchard, pp. 111–123. Federal Emergency Management Agency (FEMA), Emmitsburg, Maryland.

Hoagland, Alison K.

2010 *Mine Towns: Buildings for Workers in Michigan's Copper Country.* University of Minnesota Press, Minneapolis.

Hodder, Ian

2010 Cultural Heritage Rights: From Ownership and Descent to Justice and Well-Being. *Anthropological Quarterly* 83(4):861–882.

Hoffmann, Hillary M.

2016 Fracking the Sacred: Resolving the Tension between Unconventional Oil and Gas Development and Tribal Cultural Resources. Vermont Law School Research Paper No. 6-16.

Holmes, Douglas R., and George E. Marcus

2007 Cultures of Expertise and the Management of Globalization: Toward the Re-Functioning of Ethnography. In *Global Assemblages: Technology, Politics, and Ethics as Anthropological Problems,* edited by A. Ong and S. J. Collier, pp. 236–237. Blackwell, Oxford.

Howitt, Richard

1992 Weipa: Industrialsation and Indigenous Rights in a Remote Australian Mining Area. *Geography* 3(77):223.235.

Howitt, Richard, John Connell, and Philip Hirsch

1996 Resources, Nations and Indigenous Peoples. In *Resources, Nations and Indigenous Peoples: Case Studies from Australasia,* edited by Richard Howitt, John Connell, and Philip Hirsch, pp. 1–30. Oxford University Press, Melbourne.

Hueneke, Hannah

2006 To Climb or Not to Climb? "The Sacred Deed Done at Australia's Mighty Heart." Unpublished honours' paper, School of Resources, Environment and Society, Australian National University, Canberra.

Hughes, Lotte

2006 *Moving the Maasai: A Colonial Misadventure.* Palgrave Macmillan, London.

ICMM (International Council on Mining and Metals)

2012   *10 Principles: Sustainable Development Framework.* https://www.icmm.com/our-work/sustainable-development-framework/10-principles, accessed June 15, 2015.

2013   *Identifying Potential Overlap between Extractive Industries (Mining, Oil and Gas) and Natural World Heritage Sites.* Final report. 12 December. http://www.icmm.com/website/publications/pdfs/6950.pdf, accessed June 15, 2014.

Igoe, Jim

2004   *Conservation and Globalization: A Study of the National Parks and Indigenous Communities from East Africa to South Dakota.* Thomson/Wadsworth, Belmont, Calif.

Inglis, David, and John Bone

2006   Boundary Maintenance, Border Crossing and the Nature/Culture Divide. *European Journal of Social Theory* 9(2):272–287.

Ingold, Tim

1993   The Temporality of the Landscape. *World Archaeology* 25(2):152–174.

1995   Building, Dwelling, Living: How Animals and People Make Themselves at Home in the World. In *Shifting Contexts: Transformations in Anthropological Knowledge*, edited by M. Strathern, pp. 57–80. Routledge, London.

2000   *The Perception of the Environment: Essays on Livelihood, Dwelling and Skill.* Routledge, London.

Ingram, Jane Carter, Kent H. Redford, and James E. M. Watson

2012   Applying Ecosystem Services Approaches for Biodiversity Conservation: Benefits and Challenges. *S.A.P.I.E.N.S [Online]* 5(1).

IUCN (International Union for Conservation and Nature)

1987   *World Heritage Nomination for Uluṟu Kata Tjuṯa National Park, IUCN Summary.* Manuscript on file at the World Heritage Centre Archives, Paris.

Jackson, Antoinette T.

2012   *Speaking for the Enslaved: Heritage Interpretation at Antebellum Plantation Sites.* Left Coast Press, Walnut Creek, Calif.

Jacobson, Esther

1993   *The Deer Goddess of Ancient Siberia: A Study in the Ecology of Belief.* Brill, Leiden.

Jakle, John A.

1987   *The Visual Elements of Landscape.* University of Massachusetts Press, Amherst.

Jasinski, Marek E., Marianne N. Soleim, and Leiv Sem

2009   Painful Heritage: Cultural Landscapes of the Second World War in Norway: A New Approach. In *Proceedings of the 10th Nordic TAG Conferences at Stiklesad, Norway, 2009, BAR International Series 2399*, edited by R. Berge, M. E. Jasinski, and K. Sognnes, pp. 263–272. Archaeopress, Oxford.

Jesperson, Michele M., and Kristen Griffin

1992   *An Evaluation of Archaeological Injury Documentation "Exxon Valdez Oil Spill."* Prepared at the direction of the Comprehensive Environmental Response, Compensation, and Liability Act, and the Archaeological Steering Committee, Exxon Cultural Resource Program Files.

Johnson, David K., and Laura R. Rustin

2013   *Bibliography of "Exxon Valdez" Oil Spill Publications.* Cambridge University Press, Cambridge.

Kenzer, Martin S.
1985   Milieu and the "Intellectual Landscape": Carl O. Sauer's Undergraduate Heritage. *Annals of the Association of American Geographers* 75(2):258–270.

Kercher, Bruce
2002   Native Title in the Shadows: The Origins of the Myth of *Terra Nullius* in Early New South Wales Courts. In *Colonialism and the Modern World: Selected Studies*, edited by G. Blue, M. P. Bunton, and R. C. Croizier, pp. 100–119. M. E. Sharpe, Armonk, N.Y.

Kerle, J. Anne
1993   Historical Survey of the Vertebrate Fauna in the Vicinity of Uluṟu and Kata Tjuṯa. In *Uluṟu Fauna: The Distribution and Abundance of Vertebrate Fauna of Uluṟu (Ayers Rock-Mount Olga) National Park, NT*, edited by J. R.W. Reid, J. A. Kerle, and S. R. Morton, pp. 23–40. Australian National Parks and Wildlife Service, Canberra.

Kerwin, Dale
2006   Aboriginal Dreaming Tracks or Trading Paths: The Common Ways. Unpublished Ph.D. dissertation, Griffith University, Brisbane.

Kirmayer, Laurence
2004   Comments: An Anthropology of Structural Violence. *Current Anthropology* 45(3): 305–325.

Kirsch, Stuart
2001   Lost Worlds: Environmental Disaster, "Culture Loss," and the Law. *Current Anthropology* 42(2):167–198.
2006   *Reverse Anthropology: Indigenous Analysis of Social and Environmental Relations in New Guinea*. Stanford University Press, Stanford.
2014   *Mining Capitalism: The Relationship between Corporations and their Critics*. University of California Press, Oakland.

Kirshenblatt-Gimblett, Barbara
1995   Theorizing Heritage. *Ethnomusicology* 39(3):367–380.
2004   Intangible Heritage as Metacultural Production. *Museum International* 56(1–2):52–65.

Knapp, A. Bernard, and Wendy Ashmore
1999   Archaeological Landscapes: Constructed, Conceptualized, Ideational. In *Archaeologies of Landscape: Contemporary Perspectives*, edited by A. Bernard Knapp and Wendy Ashmore, pp. 1–30. Blackwell, Malden, Mass.

Kohen, J. L.
2003   Knowing Country: Indigenous Australians and the Land. In *Nature across Cultures: Views of Nature and Environment in Non-Western Cultures*, edited by H. Selin, pp. 226–243. Kluwer Academic, Boston.

Kopnina, Helen
2012   Toward Conservational Anthropology: Addressing Anthropocentric Bias in Anthropology. *Dialectical Anthropology* 36(1):127–146.

Kwaymullina, Ambelin, Blaze Kwaymullina, and Lauren Butterly
2015   Opportunity Lost: Changes to Aboriginal Heritage Law in Western Australia. *Indigenous Law Bulletin* 8(16):24–27.

Labadi, Sophia
2007   Representations of the Nation and Cultural Diversity in Discourses on World Heritage. *Journal of Social Archaeology* 7(2):147–170.

Lakoff, Andrew
2008   The Generic Biothreat, or, How We Became Unprepared. *Cultural Anthropology* 23(3): 399–428.
Lane, Paul
2015   Primordial Conservationists, Environmental Sustainability, and the Rhetoric of Pastoralist Cultural Heritage in East Africa. In *Heritage Keywords: Rhetoric and Redescription in Cultural Heritage,* edited by K. Lafrenze Samuels and T. Rico, pp. 259–284. University of Colorado Press, Boulder.
Langton, Marcia
2012   *The Global Mining Boom and Indigenous People: Legal and Economic Dimensions.* Routledge, London.
2013   *Boyer Lectures 2012: The Quiet Revolution: Indigenous People and the Resources Boom.* ABC Books, Sydney.
Langton, Marcia, and Judy Longbottom
2012   *Foundations for Indigenous Peoples in the Global Mining Boom.* Routledge, London.
Latour, Bruno, and Steve Woolgar
1979   *Laboratory Life: The Construction of Scientific Facts.* Sage, Beverly Hills, Calif.
Laurie, Victoria
2014   Ancient Aboriginal Sites at Risk in the Pilbara. *The Australian,* 25 September:3–4 Sydney.
Layton, Robert
1986   *Uluṟu: An Aboriginal History of Ayers Rock.* Australian Institute of Aboriginal Studies, Canberra.
1995   Relating to Country in the Western Desert. In *The Anthropology of Landscape: Perspectives on Place and Space,* edited by E. Hirsch and M. O'Hanlon, pp. 210–231. Clarendon Press, Oxford.
LeMenager, Stephanie
2014   *Living Oil: Petroleum Culture in the American Century.* Oxford University Press, New York.
Lilley, Ian
2009   Strangers and Brothers? Heritage, Human Rights and a Cosmopolitan Archaeology in Oceania. In *Cosmopolitan Archaeologies,* edited by L. Meskell, pp. 48–67. Duke University Press, Durham, N.C.
Logan, William
2007   Closing Pandora's Box: Human Rights in Conundrums in Cultural Heritage Protection. In *Cultural Heritage and Human Rights,* edited by Helaine Silverman and D. Fairchild Ruggles, pp. 33–52. New York, Springer.
Logan, William, Máiréad Nic Craith, and Ullrich Kockel (editors)
2015   *A Companion to Heritage Studies.* Wiley Blackwell, Malden, Mass.
Logan, William, and Keir Reeves (editors)
2008   *Places of Pain and Shame: Dealing with "Difficult Heritage."* Routledge, London.
Lokan, Andrew
1999   From Recognition to Reconciliation: The Functions of Aboriginal Rights Law. *Melbourne University Law Review* 23(1):65–120.

Long, Darrin Lee

2000   Cultural Heritage Management in Post-colonial Polities: Not the Heritage of the Other. *International Journal of Heritage Studies* 6(4):317–322.

Lopez, Barry

2001   The Naturalist. *Orion.* https://orionmagazine.org/article/the-naturalist, accessed June 5, 2015.

Low, Setha M., and Denise Lawrence-Zúñiga (editors)

2003   *The Anthropology of Space and Place: Locating Culture.* Blackwell, Malden, Mass.

Lowenthal, David

1998   *The Heritage Crusade and the Spoils of History.* Cambridge University Press, Cambridge.

2005   Natural and Cultural Heritage. *International Journal of Heritage Studies* 11(1):81–92.

Luke, Christina, and Morag Kersel

2013   *U.S. Cultural Diplomacy and Archaeology: Soft Power, Hard Heritage.* Routledge, New York.

Luning, Sabine

2012   Corporate Social Responsibility (CSR) for Exploration: Consultants, Companies and Communities in Processes of Engagements. *Resources Policy* 37(2):205–211.

Macdonald, Sharon

2009   *Difficult Heritage: Negotiating the Nazi Past in Nuremberg and Beyond.* Routledge, New York.

MacKinnon, J. B.

2015   Facing Fear. *Orion Magazine* 2:1–7.

Maharaj, Brij, and Meghan Crosby

2013   So What's New? Post-Apartheid Evictions, Displacement and Forced Removals. *Proceedings of the Life in a Changing Urban Landscape: Proceedings of the IGU Urban Geography Commission,* pp. 111–128. Johannesburg and Stellenbosch.

Mason, Arthur, and Maria Stoilkova

2012   Corporeality of Consultant Expertise in Arctic Natural Gas Development. *Journal of Northern Studies* 6(2):83–96.

Mathers, Clay, Timothy Darvill, and Barbara Little (editors)

2004   *Heritage of Value, Archaeology of Renown: Reshaping Archaeological Assessment and Significance.* University Press of Florida, Gainesville.

McCarthy, Cormac

1995   *The Crossing.* Vintage Books, New York.

McDonald, Jo, and Peter Veth

2009   Dampier Archipelago Petroglyphs: Archaeology, Scientific Values and National Heritage Listing. *Archaeology in Oceania* 44(S1):49–69.

Meany, Edmond S.

1906   Alaskan Mummies. *Washington Magazine* 1:1459–1468.

Meskell, Lynn

2005   Sites of Violence: Terrorism, Tourism and Heritage in the Archaeological Present. In *Embedding Ethics,* edited by L. Meskell and P. Pels, pp. 23–146. Berg, New York.

2009   *Cosmopolitan Archaeologies.* Duke University Press, Durham, N.C.

2010 Human Rights and Heritage Ethics. *Anthropological Quarterly* 83(4):839–859.

2012a *The Nature of Heritage in the New South Africa.* Wiley Blackwell, Malden, Mass.

2012b The Rush to Inscribe: Reflections on the 35th Session of the World Heritage Committee, UNESCO Paris, 2011. *Journal of Field Archaeology* 37(2):145–151.

2013 UNESCO's World Heritage Convention at 40: Challenging the Economic and Political Order of International Heritage Conservation. *Current Anthropology* 54(4):483–494.

2015a Gridlock: UNESCO, Global Conflict and Failed Ambitions. *World Archaeology* 47(2):225–238.

2015b Heritage and Cosmopolitanism. In *Blackwell Companion Guide to the New Heritage Studies*, edited by William Logan, Máiréad Nic Craith, and Ullrich Kockel, pp. 479–490. Wiley Blackwell, Malden, Mass.

2016 World Heritage and WikiLeaks: Territory, Trade, and Temples on the Thai-Cambodian Border. *Current Anthropology* 57(1):72–95.

Milcu, Andra Iaona, Jan Hanspach, David Abson, and Joern Fischer

2013 Cultural Ecosystem Services: A Literature Review and Prospects for Future Research. *Ecology and Society* 18(3):44–78.

Mobley, Charles M.

1990 *The 1989 "Exxon Valdez" Cultural Resource Program.* Exxon Shipping Company, Anchorage.

Monastersky, Richard

2015 Anthropocene: The Human Age. *Nature* 519(7542):144–147.

Moore, Donald S., Jake Koseck, and Anand Pandian (editors)

2003 *Race, Nature, and the Politics of Difference.* Duke University Press, Durham, N.C.

Moreton-Robinson, Aileen

2003 I Still Call Australia Home: Indigenous Belonging and Place in a White Postcolonizing Society. In *Whitening Race: Essays in Social and Cultural Criticism*, edited by S. Ahmed, C. Castañeda, A. M. Fortier, and M. Sheller, pp. 75–88. Aboriginal Studies Press, Canberra.

Morrison, Eric

1993 *Tatitlek.* Minerals Management Service, Social Indicators Study of Alaskan Coastal Villages: IV Postspill Key Informant Summaries, Schedule C Communities, Part I (OCS Study MMS 92-0052). U.S. Department of the Interior, Anchorage.

Mountford, Charles P.

1965 *Ayers Rock: Its People, Their Beliefs, and Their Art.* Angus and Robertson, Sydney.

Mulvaney, Ken

2013 Half a Century 40,000 Years of Culture: The Industrialisation of the Pilbara. *Artlink* 33(4):16.

Myers, Fred R.

1982 Always Ask: Resource Use and Land Ownership Among Pintupi Aborigines of the Australian Western Desert. In *Resource Managers: North America and Australia Hunter-Gatherers*, edited by N. Williams and E. Hunn, pp. 173–195. Westview, Boulder.

Nader, Laura

1972 Up the Anthropologist: Perspectives Gained from Studying Up. In *Reinventing Anthropology*, edited by D. Hymes, pp. 284–311. Pantheon, New York.

Näser, Claudia, and Cornelia Kleinitz

2012   The Good, the Bad and the Ugly: A Case Study on the Politicisation of Archaeology and Its Consequences from Northern Sudan. In *"Nihna nâs al-bahar–We are the people of the river": Ethnographic Research in the Fourth Nile Cataract Region, Sudan*, edited by C. Kleinitz and C. Näser, pp. 269–304. Meroitica 26. Wiesbaden: Harrassowitz.

Ndoro, Webber

2015   World Heritage Sites in Africa: What Are the Benefits of Nomination and Inscription? In *A Companion to Heritage Studies*, edited by William Logan, Máiréad Nic Craith, and Ullrich Kockel, pp. 392–409. Wiley Blackwell, Malden, Mass.

Ndoro, Webber, and Gamina Wijesuriya

2015   Heritage Management and Conservation: From Colonization to Globalization. In *Global Heritage: A Reader*, edited by L. Meskell, pp. 131–149. Wiley Blackwell, Malden, Mass.

Neumann, Roderick P.

1998   *Imposing Wilderness: Struggles over Livelihood and Nature Preservation in Africa.* University of California Press, Berkeley.

Nie, Martin

2006   Governing the Tongass: National Forest Conflict and Political Decision-Making. *Environmental Law* (36):385–480.

Oates, John

1999   *Myth and Reality in the Rain Forest: How Conservation Strategies Are Failing in West Africa.* University of California Press, Berkeley.

Oliver-Smith, Anthony

1996   Anthropological Research on Hazards and Disasters. *Annual Review of Anthropology* 25:303–328.

2006   Communities after Catastrophe: Reconstructing the Material, Reconstituting the Social. In *Community Building in the Twenty-First Century,* edited by Stanley E. Hyland, pp. 45–70. School of American Research Press, Santa Fe, New Mexico.

Oliver-Smith, Anthony (editor)

2009   *Development and Dispossession: The Crisis of Forced Displacement and Resettlement.* School for Advanced Research Press, Sante Fe.

Olsen, Bjørnar, and Þóra Pétursdóttir

2014   Imaging Modern Decay: The Aesthetics of Ruin Photography. *Journal of Contemporary Archaeology* 1(1):7–23.

Olwig, Kenneth R.

1996   Recovering the Substantive Nature of Landscape. *Annals of the Association of American Geographers* 86(4):630–653.

2004   "This Is Not a Landscape": Circulating Reference and Land Shaping. In *European Rural Landscapes: Persistence and Change in a Globalising Environment,* edited by H. Palang, H. Sooväli, M. Antrop, and G. Setten, pp. 41–66. Kluwer Academic, Dordrecht.

Ong, Aiwa, and John Collier (editors)

2007   *Global Assemblages: Technology, Politics, and Ethics as Anthropological Problems.* Blackwell, Oxford.

Peterson, Nicolas, and Will Sanders
1998   *Citizenship and Indigenous Australians: Changing Conceptions and Possibilities.* Cambridge University Press, Cambridge.

Phillimore, John
2014   The Politics of Resource Development in Western Australia. In *Resource Curse or Cure? On the Sustainability of Development in Western Australia,* edited by M. Brueckner, A. Durey, R. Mayes, and C. Pforr, pp. 25–40. Springer, London.

Pilbara Regional Council
2014   *Council Agenda.* 9 June. http://www.prc.wa.gov.au/wp-content/uploads/2015/01/PRC-Council-Agenda-20140609.pdf, accessed June 15, 2014.

Plets, Gertjan, Wouter Gheyle, Ruth Plets, Eduard Pavlovich Dvornikov, and Jean Bourgeois
2011   A Line through the Sacred Lands of the Altai Mountains: Perspectives on the Altai Pipeline Project. *Mountain Research and Development* 31(4):372–379.

Povinelli, Elizabeth A.
2002   *The Cunning of Recognition: Indigenous Alterities and the Making of Australian Multiculturalism.* Duke University Press, Durham, N.C.

Pretty, Jules, Bill Adams, Fikret Berkes, S. de Athayde, Nigel Dudley, Eugene Hunn, Luisa Maffi, Kay Milton, David Rapport, and Paul Robbins
2009   The Intersections of Biological Diversity and Cultural Diversity: Towards Integration. *Conservation and Society* 7(2):100–112.

Prosper, Lisa
2007   Wherein Lies the Heritage Value? Rethinking Heritage Value of Cultural Landscapes from an Aboriginal Perspective. *George Wright Forum* 24(2):117–124.

Quivik, Frederic L.
2007   The Historical Significance of Tailings and Slag: Industrial Waste as Cultural Resource. *Society for Industrial Archaeology* 33(2):35–52.

Rajak, Dinah
2011   *In Good Company: An Anatomy of Corporate Social Responsibility.* Stanford University Press, Stanford.

Redford, Kent H., and Steven E. Sanderson
2000   Extracting Humans from Nature. *Conservation Biology* 14(5):1362–1364.

Reedy-Maschner, Katherine L., and Herbert D. G. Maschner
2013   Sustaining Sanak Island, Alaska: A Cultural Land Trust. *Sustainability* 5(10):4406–4427.

Reger, Douglas R.
1998   Archeology of the Northern Kenai Peninsula and Upper Cook Inlet. *Arctic Anthropology* 35(1):160–171.

Reger, Douglas R., Debra Corbett, Amy Steffian, Patrick Saltonstall, Ted Birkedal, and Linda Finn Yarborough
2000   *Archeological Index Site Monitoring: Final Report.* Alaska Department of Natural Resources, Division of Parks and Outdoor Recreation, Office of History and Archaeology, Anchorage.

Reid, J. R. W., J. A. Kerle, and S. A. Morton
1993   *Uluṟu Fauna: The Distribution and Abundance of Vertebrate Fauna of Uluṟu (Ayers*

Rock-Mount Olga) National Park, NT. Australian National Parks and Wildlife Service, Canberra.

Rico, Trinidad

2008   Negative Heritage: The Place of Conflict in World Heritage. *Conservation and Management of Archaeological Sites* 10(4):344–352.

Ringer, Greg (editor)

2013   *Destinations: Cultural Landscapes of Tourism.* Routledge, London.

Rojek, Chris, and John Urry (editors)

1997   *Touring Cultures: Transformations of Travel and Theory.* Routledge, London.

Rose, Bruce

1995   *Land Management Issues: Attitudes and Perceptions amongst Aboriginal People of Central Australia.* Central Land Council, Alice Springs.

Rose, Deborah Bird

1996   *Nourishing Terrains: Australian Aboriginal Views of Landscape and Wilderness.* Australian Heritage Commission, Canberra.

Rosenfeld, Andrée

1989   Rock-Art Research: World Congress in Australia. *Current Anthropology* 30(3):410–411.

Rudaya, N., P. Tarasov, N. Dorofeyuk, N. Solovieva, I. Kalugin, A. Andreev, A. Daryin, B. Diekmann, F. Riedel, N. Tserendash, and M. Wagner

2009   Holocene Environments and Climate in the Mongolian Altai Reconstructed from the Hoton-Nur Pollen and Diatom Records: A Step towards Better Understanding Climate Dynamics in Central Asia. *Quaternary Science Reviews* 28(5–6):540–554.

Ruru, Jacinta

2009   Property Rights and Maori: A Right to Own a River? *Proceedings of the New Zealand Centre for Environmental Law Conference.* University of Otago, Dunedin.

Said, Edward

1979   *Orientalism.* Vintage Books, New York.

Sauer, Carl O.

1925   The Morphology of Landscapes. *University of California Publications in Geography* 2:19–54.

Saulitis, Eva

2013   *Into Great Silence: A Memoir of Discovery and Loss among Vanishing Orcas.* Beacon Press, Boston.

Sawyer, Suzana

2004   *Crude Chronicles: Indigenous Politics, Multinational Oil, and Neoliberalism in Ecuador.* Duke University Press, Durham, N.C.

Scambary, Benedict

2013   *My Country, Mine Country: Indigenous People, Mining and Development Contestation in Remote Australia.* Australian National University E Press, Canberra.

Scham, Sandra

2009   Diplomacy and Desired Pasts. *Journal of Social Archaeology* 9(2):163–199.

Schama, Simon

1996   *Landscape and Memory.* Knopf, New York.

Schmidt, Peter R.
2006   *Historical Archaeology in Africa: Representation, Social Memory, and Oral Traditions.* AltaMira Press, Lanham, Md.

Schmidt, Peter R., and Thomas Carl Patterson (editors)
1995   *Making Alternative Histories: The Practice of Archaeology and History in Non-Western Settings.* School of American Research Press, Sante Fe.

Schofield, John (editor)
2014   *Who Needs Experts? Counter-Mapping Cultural Heritage.* Ashgate, Farnham.

Schröter, Matthias, Emma H. Zanden, Alexander P. E. Oudenhoven, Roy P. Remme, Hector M. Serna-Chavez, Rudolf S. Groot, and Paul Opdam
2014   Ecosystem Services as a Contested Concept: A Synthesis of Critique and Counter-Arguments. *Conservation Letters* 7(6):514–523.

Seagle, Caroline
2012   Inverting the Impacts: Mining, Conservation and Sustainability Claims near the Rio Tinto/QMM Ilmenite Mine in Southeast Madagascar. *Journal of Peasant Studies* 39(2):447–477.

See, Scott F.
2013   Keweenaw National Historical Park: Heritage Partnerships in an Industrial Landscape. Unpublished Ph.D. dissertation, Department of Social Sciences, Michigan Technological University, Houghton.

Shackel, Paul A.
2011   Pursuing Heritage, Engaging Communities. *Historical Archaeology* 45(1):1–9.

Shamir, Ronen
2004   Between Self-Regulation and the Alien Tort Claims Act: On the Contested Concept of Corporate Social Responsibility. *Law & Society Review* 38(4):635–664.
2010   Capitalism, Governance, and Authority: The Case of Corporate Social Responsibility. *Annual Review of Law and Social Science* (6):531–553.

Sharp, Nonie
2002   *Saltwater People: The Waves of Memory.* University of Toronto Press, Toronto.

Shepherd, Nick, and Alejandro Haber
2011   What's Up with WAC? Archaeology and "Engagement" in a Globalized World. *Public Archaeology* 10(2):96–115.

Silberman, Neil A.
2015   Heritage Places: Evolving Conceptions and Changing Forms. In *A Companion to Heritage Studies*, edited by William Logan, Máiréad Nic Craith, and Ullrich Kockel, pp. 29–40. Wiley Blackwell, Malden, Mass.

Silverman, Helaine
2011   Border Wars: The Ongoing Temple Dispute between Thailand and Cambodia and UNESCOs World Heritage List. *International Journal of Heritage Studies* 17(1):1–21.

Silverman, Helaine, and D. Fairchild Ruggles
2007   Cultural Heritage and Human Rights. In *Cultural Heritage and Human Rights*, edited by Helaine Silverman and D. Fairchild Ruggles, pp. 3–29. Springer, New York.

Slater, Candace
2002   *Entangled Edens: Visions of the Amazon.* University of California Press, Berkeley.

Smith, Anita
2015   (Re)visioning the Maʻohi Landscape of Marae Taputapuatea, French Polynesia: World Heritage and Indigenous Knowledge Systems in the Pacific Islands. In A *Companion to Heritage Studies*, edited by William Logan, Máiréad Nic Craith, and Ullrich Kockel, pp. 101–114. Wiley Blackwell, Malden, Mass.

Smith, Claire
2011   Errors of Fact and Errors of Representation: Response to Shepherd and Haber's Critique of the World Archaeological Congress. *Public Archaeology* 10(4):223–234.

Smith, Laurajane
2004   *Archaeological Theory and the Politics of Cultural Heritage.* Routledge, London.
2006   *The Uses of Heritage.* Routledge, London.

Smith, L. Tuhiwai
1999   *Decolonizing Methodologies: Research and Indigenous Peoples.* Zed Books, London.

Solli, Brit, Mats Burström, Ewa Domanska, Matt Edgeworth, Alfredo González-Ruibal, Cornelius Holtorf, Gavin Lucas, Terje Oestigaard, Laurajane Smith, and Christopher Witmore
2011   Some Reflections on Heritage and Archaeology in the Anthropocene. *Norwegian Archaeological Review* 44(1):40–88.

Somerville, Margaret
2013   *Water in a Dry Land: Place-Learning through Art and Story.* Routledge, New York.

Spriggs, Ebonnie, and Lucie Bell
2015   Widespread Redundancies in Mining, Oil and Gas Industries Impact Resource-Reliant Towns in WA's Pilbara. ABC News, 26 March. http://www.abc.net.au/news/2015-03-26/mining-redundancies-hitting-the-pilbara-region/6349700, accessed June 15, 2015.

Stilgoe, John R.
1982   *Common Landscapes of America, 1580–1845.* Yale University Press, New Haven.

Stone, Philip, and Richard Sharpley
2008   Consuming Dark Tourism: A Thanatological Perspective. *Annals of Tourism Research* 35(2):574–595.

Strack, Mick
2014   "They'll Be Drownded in the Tide": Reconsidering Coastal Boundaries in the Face of Sea-Level Rise. *Geography Research Forum* 34:23–39.

Sutton, Peter
2003   *Native Title in Australia: An Ethnographic Perspective.* Cambridge University Press, Cambridge.

Swanepoel, Esmarie
2015   WA Oil and Gas Jobs Loom, Woodside Confirms Cuts. *Mining Weekly*, 25 March. http://www.miningweekly.com/article/wa-oil-and-gas-job-losses-loom-woodside-confirms-cuts-2015-03-25, accessed June 15, 2015.

Swidler, Nina, Kurt E. Dongoske, Roger Anyon, and Alan S. Downer (editors)
1997   *Native Americans and Archaeologists: Stepping Stones to Common Ground.* AltaMira Press, Walnut Creek, Calif.

Taçon, Paul S.
1999   Identifying Ancient Sacred Landscapes in Australia: From Physical to Social. In *Ar-*

chaeologies of Landscape: Contemporary Perspectives, edited by Wendy Ashmore and A. Bernard Knapp, pp. 33–57. Blackwell, Malden, Mass.

Tapsell, Paul

1997 The Flight of the Pareraututu: An Investigation of Taonga from a Tribal Perspective. *Journal of Polynesian Society* (106):323–374.

Taylor, Diana

2003 *The Archive and the Repertoire: Performing Cultural Memory in the Americas.* Duke University Press, Durham, N.C.

Taylor, John

2009 Data Mining: Indigenous Peoples, Applied Demography and the Resource Extraction Industry. In *Power, Culture, Economy: Indigenous Australians and Mining*, edited by J. C. Altman and D. Martin, pp. 51–72. Australian National University E Press, Canberra.

Taylor, Ken, and Jane Lennon

2011 Cultural Landscapes: A Bridge between Culture and Nature? *International Journal of Heritage Studies* 17(6):537–554.

2012 *Managing Cultural Landscapes.* Routledge, London.

Terborgh, John

2000 The Fate of Tropical Forests: A Matter of Stewardship. *Conservation Biology* 14(5): 1358–1361.

Tilley, Christopher

1994 *A Phenomenology of Landscape: Places, Paths and Monuments.* Berg, Oxford.

Tilt, Bryan

2015 *Dams and Development in China: The Moral Economy of Water and Power.* Columbia University Press, New York.

Timothy, Dallen J.

2011 *Cultural Heritage and Tourism: An Introduction.* Channel View Publications, Minneapolis.

Titchen, Sarah M.

2013 On the Construction of "Outstanding Universal Value": Some Comments on the Implementation of the 1972 UNESCO World Heritage Convention. *Conservation and Management of Archaeological Sites* 1(4):235–242.

Tsing, Anna Lowenhaupt

2003 Natural Resources and Capitalist Frontiers. *Economic and Political Weekly* 38(48): 5100–5106.

2005 *Friction: An Ethnography of Global Connection.* Princeton University Press, Princeton, N.J.

Tuan, Yi-Fu

1977 *Space and Place: The Perspective of Experience.* University of Minnesota Press, Minneapolis.

Turtinen, Jan

2000 *Globalising Heritage: On UNESCO and the Transnational Construction of a World Heritage.* Stockholm Center for Organizational Research, Stockholm.

Uluṟu-Kata Tjuṯa Board of Management

2009 *Uluṟu-Kata Tjuṯa National Park Draft Plan of Management.* Commonwealth of Australia, Yulara.

UNESCO (United Nations Educational, Scientific and Cultural Organization)

1987   *Report of the World Heritage Committee. Eleventh Session, Paris, France.* http://whc. unesco.org/en/sessions/11COM, accessed October 2014.

2008   *Sustainable Tourism and the Preservation of the World Heritage Site of the Ifugao Rice Terraces Philippines.* http://www.unescobkk.org/en/culture/our-projects/sustainable-cultural-tourism-and-ecotourism/impact/new-impact-publications/ifugao-rice-terraces, accessed October 2014.

UNHRC (United Nations Human Rights Council)

2011   State of the World's Minorities and Indigenous Peoples 2011, Mongolia. http://www. refworld.org/docid/4e16d36711.html, accessed May 25, 2014.

U.S. Department of State

2014   *The New Silk Road Post-2014: Challenges and Opportunities.* http://www.state.gov/p/ sca/rls/rmks/2015/236214.htm, accessed June 8, 2015.

Veth, Peter

2015   Exile in the Kingdom: The Struggle for Cultural Heritage in the Pilbara. In *Cultural Anthropology*, 17 December. https://culanth.org/fieldsights/762-exile-in-the-king-dom-the-struggle-for-cultural-heritage-in-the-pilbara, accessed May 16, 2017.

Watson, Irene

2002   Buried Alive. *Law and Critique* 13(3):253–269.

2009   Sovereign Spaces: Caring for Country and the Homeless Position of Aboriginal Peoples. *South Atlantic Quarterly* 108(1):27–51.

Weiner, James F., and Katie Glaskin

2007   Customary Land Tenure and Registration in Papua New Guinea and Australia: Anthropological Perspectives. In *Customary Land Tenure and Registration in Papua New Guinea and Australia: Anthropological Perspectives*, edited by James F. Weiner and Katie Glaskin, pp. 1–14. Australian National University E Press, Canberra.

Weiss, Lindsay M.

2009   Fictive Capital and Economies of Desire: A Case Study of Illegal Diamond Buying and Apartheid Landscapes in 19th Century Southern Africa. Unpublished Ph.D. dissertation, Department of Anthropology, Columbia University, New York.

2014   Informal Settlements and Urban Heritage Landscapes in South Africa. *Journal of Social Archaeology* 14(1):3–25.

Welker, Marina A.

2009   Corporate Security Begins in the Community: Mining, the Corporate Social Responsibility Industry, and Environmental Advocacy in Indonesia. *Cultural Anthropology* 24(1):142–179.

2014   *Enacting the Corporation: An American Mining Firm in Post-Authoritarian Indonesia.* University of California Press, Berkeley.

Wells, P. G., James N. Butler, and Jane S. Hughes

1995   *"Exxon Valdez" Oil Spill: Fate and Effects in Alaskan Waters.* American Society for Testing and Materials, Philadelphia.

Welsh, Peter H.

1997   The Power of Possessions: The Case against Property. *Museum Anthropology* 23(3): 12–18.

Widgren, Mats
2010   Reading the Prehistoric Landscape. *Ymer* 130:69–85.
Wiens, John A.
2013   *Oil in the Environment: Legacies and Lessons of the "Exxon Valdez" Oil Spill.* Cambridge University Press, Cambridge.
Winter, Tim
2007   *Post-Conflict Heritage, Postcolonial Tourism: Tourism, Politics and Development at Angkor.* Routledge, London.
2013   Clarifying the Critical in Critical Heritage Studies. *International Journal of Heritage Studies* 19(6):532–545.
Wooley, Christopher B.
1995   Alutiiq Culture before and after the *Exxon Valdez* Oil Spill. *American Indian Culture and Research Journal* 19(4):125–154.
Workman, William B.
1998   Archaeology of the Southern Kenai Peninsula. *Arctic Anthropology* 35(1):146–159.
World Commission on Environment and Development
1987   *Our Common Future.* Oxford University Press, Oxford.
Wylie, Alison
2002   Preface. In *Thinking from Things: Essays in the Philosophy of Archaeology,* edited by A. Wylie, pp. 1–22. University of California Press, Berkeley.
Yarborough, Linda Finn
2000   Prehistoric and Early Historic Subsistence Patterns along the North Gulf of Alaska Coast. Unpublished Ph.D. dissertation, Department of Anthropology, University of Wisconsin, Madison.
Zhan, Mei
2009   *Other-Worldly: Making Chinese Medicine through Transnational Frames.* Duke University Press, Durham, N.C.

Index

Page numbers in *italics* refer to figures and maps.

MELISSA BAIRD is associate professor of anthropology at Michigan Techno-logical University. Her research engages a forensic approach (archaeology, eth-nography, discourse analyses) that is historically grounded and ethnographi-cally informed to understand heritage in the extractive zone—the places where industries, communities, and ecologies converge.

Cultural Heritage Studies

EDITED BY PAUL A. SHACKEL, UNIVERSITY OF MARYLAND

Earth Politics and Intangible Heritage: Three Case Studies in the Americas, by Jessica Joyce Christie (2021)

Negotiating Heritage through Education and Archaeology: Colonialism, National Identity, and Resistance in Belize, by Alicia Ebbitt McGill (2021)

Baseball and Cultural Heritage, edited by Gregory Ramshaw and Sean Gammon (2022)

Conflict Archaeology, Historical Memory, and the Experience of War: Beyond the Battlefield, edited by Mark Axel Tveskov and Ashley Ann Bissonnette (2022)

www.ingramcontent.com/pod-product-compliance
Lightning Source LLC
Chambersburg PA
CBHW071104280326
41928CB00051B/2809